Death

AND·THE

Afterlife

BOOKS BY CLIFFORD A. PICKOVER

Death AND·THE Afterlife

A CHRONOLOGICAL JOURNEY From CREMATION To QUANTUM RESURRECTION

CLIFFORD A. PICKOVER

STERLING
New York

STERLING
New York

An Imprint of Sterling Publishing
1166 Avenue of the Americas
New York, NY 10036

Cover design by Spencer Charles
Interior Design by Philip Buchanan

ISBN 978-1-4549-1434-1

Distributed in Canada by Sterling Publishing
℅ Canadian Manda Group, 664 Annette Street
Toronto, Ontario, Canada M6S 2C8
Distributed in the United Kingdom by GMC Distribution Services
Castle Place, 166 High Street, Lewes, East Sussex, England BN7 1XU
Distributed in Australia by Capricorn Link (Australia) Pty. Ltd.
P.O. Box 704, Windsor, NSW 2756, Australia

For information about custom editions, special sales, and premium and corporate purchases,
please contact Sterling Special Sales at 800-805-5489 or specialsales@sterlingpublishing.com.

Manufactured in China

10 9

www.sterlingpublishing.com

"It cannot be that our life is a mere bubble, cast up by eternity to float a moment on its waves and then sink into nothingness. . . . There is a realm where the rainbow never fades, where the stars will be spread out before us like islands that slumber in the ocean, and where the beautiful beings, which now pass before us like shadows, will stay in our presence forever."

—George D. Prentice, "The Broken-Hearted,"
The Country Gentleman (vol. 4), 1854

"Life survives in the chaos of the cosmos by picking order out of the winds. Death is certain, but life becomes possible by following patterns that lead like paths of firmer ground through the swamps of time. Cycles of light and dark, of heat and cold, of magnetism, radioactivity, and gravity all provide vital guides— and life learns to respond to even their most subtle signs. . . . The breeding of a bristle worm is coordinated on the ocean floor by a glimmer of light reflected from the moon. . . . Nothing happens in isolation. We breathe and bleed, we laugh and cry, we crash and die in time with cosmic cues."

—Lyall Watson, *Supernature*, 1973

"These are the pale deaths which men miscall their lives: for all the scents of green things growing, each breath is but an exaltation of the grave. Bodies jerk like puppet corpses, and hell walks laughing."

—S. R. Donaldson, *Lord Foul's Bane*, 1977

"Life is a narrow vale between the cold and barren peaks of two eternities. We strive in vain to look beyond the heights. We cry aloud, and the only answer is the echo of our wailing cry. From the voiceless lips of the unreplying dead there comes no word; but in the night of death hope sees a star and listening love can hear the rustle of a wing."

—Robert Ingersoll (a tribute delivered at his brother's grave, 1879)

CONTENTS

INTRODUCTION

"Death is not extinguishing the light; it is putting out the lamp because dawn has come."

—Rabindranath Tagore, quoted in *Message of the East*, 1947

THROUGHOUT HISTORY, THE NATURE AND MYS-tery of death have captivated artists, scientists, philosophers, physicians, and theologians. Symbols and stories involving death permeate our great works of art, architecture, and literature—and they shape our funeral customs and preparations for the ends of our lives. Our interest in death, along with what may lie beyond, also is reflected in popular culture, with movies and books often presenting spooky or transcendent themes involving near-death experiences, the afterlife, and creatures rising from the dead. Many of these themes are ancient, hearkening back to times when people not only believed in miracles but also felt a deep connection to nature and a sense of being surrounded by unseen entities.

Welcome to *Death and the Afterlife*, in which we shed light into the darkness. Here, a topic can turn from gruesome or emotional to cosmic and transcendent with just the turn of a page. In what other book can you find a discussion of Viking ship burials alongside an entry on quantum immortality, which mysteriously suggests a way we might live forever through subatomic physics? Few books attempt to describe the wonders of Truman Capote's "grass harp"—which allows us to hear dead people in the sounds of wind-swept grass—and include an entry on electronic voice phenomena, in which people hear the dead in amplified recordings with background noise.

Each book entry is short—only a few paragraphs in length. This format allows readers to jump in to ponder a subject without having to sort through a lot of verbiage. Want to know about the Maya death gods and their necklaces of eyeballs? Turn to the entry on Xibalba for a quick adventure and a gruesome scare. Might golems or the Terra-Cotta Army ever gain a semblance of consciousness and interact with the living? Turn to the entries on these baffling "beings" for a brief introduction.

Do death's-head hawk moths and guillotines give you the creeps? What really motivated the kamikaze pilots of World War II? What are Bifrost, Summer Land, and transhumanism—and how did the ancient Natufians of the Eastern Mediterranean region change our world? Who were Elisabeth Kübler-Ross, the Witch of Endor, and Carlos Schwabe—and why did European plague doctors dress in costumes with scary birdlike beaks? Concerned about how physicians determine the moment of death or think about the ethics of euthanasia? We'll tackle these and other thought-provoking questions in the pages that follow.

Of course, my approach has some disadvantages. In just a few paragraphs, I can't go into any depth on a subject; however,

I provide suggestions for further reading in the Notes and References section, which readers interested in pursuing any subject covered in the book can employ as a useful starting point. Sometimes I quote authors or famous researchers in the entries in this book, but purely for brevity I don't list the precise source of a quote or the author's credentials. However, references in the back of the book should help make the author's identity clearer.

I have had a longtime fascination with death, dying, consciousness, the afterlife, and topics at the borderlands of science. Some of my interest was rekindled after reading freelance writer Greta Christina's 2005 essay "Comforting Thoughts about Death That Have Nothing to Do with God." Greta writes, "The fact that your life span is an infinitesimally tiny fragment in the life of the universe, that there is, at the very least, a strong possibility that when you die, you disappear completely and forever, and that in five hundred years nobody will remember you . . . [this] can make you feel erased, wipe out joy, make your life seem like ashes in your hands." And then I sigh. Greta admits that she doesn't know what happens when we die, but she doesn't think this essential mystery really matters. She reminds us that we should be happy because it is amazing that we even get a *chance* to be alive. We get to be *conscious*: "We get to be connected with each other and with the world, and we get to be aware of that connection and to spend a few years mucking about its possibilities." Her essay ends on a bright note as she enumerates items that contribute to her happiness, such as Shakespeare, sex, five-spice chicken, Thai restaurants, Louis Armstrong, and drifting patterns in the clouds.

As you read through *Death and the Afterlife*, remember that even if we may consider some of the ideas and rituals surrounding death unscientific, these are all still worthy areas of study. And the subjects we address are not all depressing. Our rituals and myths are, at minimum, fascinating models of human understanding and creativity—and of how we reach across cultures to understand one another and learn about what we hold sacred.

Our brains may be wired with a desire for magic, unseen forces and a need to exert control over the universe and have our deepest fantasies fulfilled. Perhaps our brains and cultural evolution operate in a way that predisposes us to believe in the soul, spirits, and the afterlife to foster community cohesion and create a sense of peace as the deaths of family members, and of ourselves, approach. The reasons for our fascination with death and the rituals we use to make sense of death are buried deep in the essence of our nature. Ideas about death, religion, mythology, and the afterlife are at the edges of the known and the unknown, poised on the fractal boundaries of psychology, history, philosophy, biology, and many other scientific disciplines. Humans need to make sense of the world and will surely continue to use both logic and mystical thinking for that task. What patterns and connections will we see as the twenty-first century progresses? How will we continue to cope with death—or elude death—in the future?

"Death destroys the body, as the scaffolding is destroyed after the building is up and finished. And he whose building is up rejoices at the destruction of the scaffolding and of the body."

—Leo Tolstoy, *Thoughts and Aphorisms*, 1905

ORGANIZATION AND PURPOSE OF THE BOOK

MY GOAL IN WRITING *DEATH AND THE Afterlife* is to provide a wide audience with a brief guide to curious, mystical, and important practical ideas related to death and the afterlife, with entries short enough to digest in a few minutes. We'll roam far and wide through philosophy, popular culture, science, sociology, art, and religion. The entries in this book are ones that interest me personally—for example, when I was younger, I became fascinated with writers such as H. P. Lovecraft and Edgar Allan Poe and painters such as Hugo Simberg and Carlos Schwabe. Although I try to study as many areas of science and culture as I can, it is difficult to become fluent in all aspects. This is not a comprehensive or scholarly dissertation but is intended as recreational reading. Alas, obviously not all of the great scientific, historical, and cultural concepts related to death are covered in order to prevent the book from growing too large. Thus, in contemplating the mysteries of death and the afterlife, I have been forced to omit many topics. Nevertheless, I believe that I have included many entries that have historical and cultural significance or have had a strong or curious influence on

science and societies. I welcome feedback and suggestions from readers, as I consider this an ongoing project and a labor of love.

This book is organized chronologically in accordance with the year associated with an entry. Dating of entries can be a question of judgment, and sometimes I have surveyed colleagues and other interesting thinkers and decided to use the date when a concept gained particular prominence. Many dates, of course, are highly approximate. Whenever possible, I have given at least a partial justification for the dates used.

Let's wrap up this introduction by noting that the mystery of consciousness and the nature of mind will be studied for years to come. American psychologist and neuroscientist Stephen Kosslyn has made the remarkable suggestion that "your mind may arise not simply from your own brain but from the brains of other people." He notes that all of us set up "social prosthetic systems," or SPSs, in which we rely on others to "extend our reasoning abilities and help us regulate and constructively employ our emotions." A good marriage often occurs when two people can serve as effective SPSs for each other. In some sense, we "lend" parts of our brains to others. Kosslyn concludes that your mind arises from the combined activity of your own brain and those of your SPSs. Using this line of reasoning, "one might argue that when your body dies, part of your mind may survive."

Moreover, as we age, the molecules in our bodies are constantly being exchanged with our environment. With every breath, we may be inhaling hundreds of millions of atoms of air exhaled weeks ago by someone on the other side of the planet. Thinking at a higher level, our brains and organs are "vanishing" into thin air, the cells sometimes being replaced as quickly as they are destroyed. A year or two from now, a majority of the atoms in our bodies will have been replaced with new ones. We are a seething mass of atomic and molecular trajectories that form threads in the fabric of space-time.

What does it mean that your brain may have little in common, at the molecular level, with the brain you had a few years ago? If you are something other than the collection of atoms making up your body, what are you? You are not so much your atoms as you are the *pattern* in which your atoms are arranged. People are persistent space-time tangles. It's possible that you have an atom of Jesus of Nazareth coursing through your body. Gilgamesh, the historical king who ruled the city of Uruk, could be part of your brain or tendons or heart. An atom in your retina may be in the tears of a happy lunar princess a hundred years from now. On this subject, English poet John Donne (1572–1631) wrote in "Meditation XVII" (*Devotions upon Emergent Occasions*, 1624):

" *No man is an island, entire of itself. Every man is a piece of the continent, a part of the main. If a clod be washed away by the sea, Europe is the less, as well as if a promontory were, as well as if a manor of thy friends or of thine own were. Any man's death diminishes me, because I am involved in mankind and therefore never send to know for whom the bell tolls. It tolls for thee.* "

CREMATION

RUDOLF VRBA (1924–2006), ALFRÉD WETZLER (1918–1988)

IMAGINE TWO OF THE LARGE AND FRIGHTENING crematoria used around the clock to burn and dispose of bodies during the Nazi Holocaust. According to the 1944 "Vrba–Wetzler Report," a huge chimney rose from the furnace room, around which were grouped nine furnaces, each having four openings. "Each opening can take three normal corpses at once, and after an hour and a half, the bodies are completely burned. This corresponds to a daily capacity of about 2,000 bodies. . . ." Today, for biblical and Talmudic reasons, Orthodox Judaism generally prohibits cremation (the burning of a corpse as part of a funeral or postfuneral rite); however, as a reaction to the Holocaust even some secular Jews hesitate to cremate their deceased.

Today, crematoria are often computer-controlled, and the cremated remains of our departed loved ones are not really ashes but mostly bone fragments that usually are then pulverized by a machine that creates a product with the consistency of coarse sand. Large items, such as titanium hip replacements or casket hinges, are removed before the pulverization. The remains may be kept in an urn, stored in a columbarium (a special memorial building), buried, or spread over the land or sea. One commercial service actually offers to rocket-launch a sample of the remains into space.

Buddhists, Hindus, Jains, and Sikhs make very widespread use of cremation. Open-air cremations often are practiced in India—for example, on wood-fueled pyres on the banks of the Ganges River. In contrast, the Eastern Orthodox Church and Islam forbid cremation. Christians historically have discouraged cremation, but today many denominations accept the practice.

For a quick march through history, note that cremation dates at least as far back as 20,000 BCE, the estimated date for the cremated remains of "Mungo Lady," an early human inhabitant of Australia. On the basis of her bones' burn mark patterns, scientists believe her corpse was burned, crushed, burned again, and then covered with red ocher, perhaps in a ritual to prevent her from returning to haunt them. The ancient Egyptians shunned cremation, preferring to embalm bodies to facilitate the transition to the afterlife. Homer, the ancient Greek poet, gave one of the earliest descriptions of cremation, and the ancient Romans performed cremation for their most honored citizens.

See also Mummies (c. 5050 BCE), Sky Burial (1328), Autopsy (1761), Cemeteries (1831), Embalming (1867)

Bright flames of the *Ngaben* (cremation ceremony) in Ubud, Bali. The Balinese Hindu dead often are buried for a period of time until an auspicious day, when they are placed in a coffin within a buffalo-shaped sarcophagus or a wood and papier-mâché temple structure that is carried to the cremation site and burned. The fire is believed to free the spirit and allow for reincarnation.

NATUFIAN FUNERAL FLOWERS

"EVERYTHING CHANGED WITH THE NATUFIANS," according to the Israeli archaeologist Daniel Nadel in discussing the **cemeteries** and funeral flowers of the Natufians, a people who existed from about 12,500 BCE to 9,500 BCE in the Levant region of the eastern Mediterranean. In 2013, the remains of colorful and aromatic flowers were found in Stone Age Natufian graves.

The Nuftian people existed at the cusp of the agricultural revolution, living in the earliest settlements and leaving behind some of the oldest known cemeteries. Dr. Nadel has noted that before the Natufians, it was possible to find isolated burials, but some Natufian sites have more than 100 skeletons in one confined area.

In Raqefet Cave in Mount Carmel (northern Israel), four flower-lined graves were discovered that date back to around 11,000 BCE. In particular, archaeologists found impressions of stems and flowers that are probably from sage, figwort, and mint plants. Nadel and colleagues conclude from these flowers, "Grave preparation was a sophisticated planned process, embedded with social and spiritual meanings reflecting a complex pre-agricultural society undergoing profound changes at the end of the Pleistocene." Although there are potentially older suggestions of funeral flowers in the form of pollen found in a 70,000-year-old grave of a Neanderthal in Iraq, some scientists argued that rats may have stored seeds and flowers in that ancient grave.

Archaeologists also have found that the Natufians made feasting part of some funerals—yet another indication of a special, socially related treatment of the dead. For example, the grave of a Natufian woman was discovered that contained the blackened shells of dozens of tortoises, which may have been brought to the site and eaten during a feast related to a funeral. Some Natufian burials also have been marked by hollowed stone "pipes" that possibly served as a kind of tombstone. During the Late Natufian period, skulls sometimes were removed, and the separated crania were found in separate caches and/or domestic locales.

See also Burial Mounds (c. 4000 BCE), Gravestones (c. 1600 BCE), Funeral Processions (c. 1590), Cemeteries (1831)

Human remains from a Natufian burial inside Raqefet Cave in Mount Carmel (northern Israel). (Photo by Dani Nadel.)

MUMMIES

FOR THOUSANDS OF YEARS, HUMANS HAVE BEEN concerned with body decomposition after death, and many cultures took steps to resist such decay. Egyptian mummies in their linen wrappings are among the most notable examples of such a pervasive concern with death and preparations for life beyond death. However, the term *mummy* has much a broader scope and is used to refer to bodies that have been either intentionally or accidentally preserved by exposure to cold, submersion in bogs, treatment with chemicals and drying agents, and so forth. The oldest known deliberately created mummy is of a child from the South American Chinchorro culture dated to around 5050 BCE, possibly several centuries before the earliest Egyptian mummies. Chinchorro people had several techniques for making mummies, one of which involved removing the head, arms, and legs from the trunk; disemboweling the corpse; and then reattaching the pieces. Sometimes the body was reinforced and strengthened with sticks or covered with mud that was sculpted into a human form. Partly because these mummies often were repainted and showed signs of wear, there is speculation that they were kept as household statues.

The Egyptians removed the brain from many of their mummy preparations through the nostrils, and most other organs also were removed, except for the heart. Naturally occurring salts such as natron were used to remove moisture from the body. In the Middle Ages and even more recently, powder made from mummy bodies was used in some medical treatments.

Mummies formed through natural processes are common and include famous figures such as Ötzi the Iceman, who was discovered in the cold Alps mountain range and dated to about 3300 BCE, and bog bodies found in northern European peat bogs that contain dead plant materials, such as mosses, with conditions that often include acidic water, low temperatures, and low oxygen. Today, methods such as plastination can be used to preserve bodies in a process in which water and fat are replaced by certain plastics.

See also Cremation (c. 20,000 BCE), *The Egyptian Book of the Dead* (c. 1550 BCE), Terra-Cotta Army (c. 210 BCE), Sky Burial (1328), Embalming (1867), Death Mask (c. 1888), Cryonics (1962)

Preserved mummies of former chiefs appear in some village huts in West Papua's Baliem Valley.

BURIAL MOUNDS

THOMAS JEFFERSON (1743–1826)

THE GREAT OLD ENGLISH EPIC POEM *BEOWULF* (possibly composed as far back as the eighth century) concludes with the death of the hero Beowulf, along with poignant instructions left by him as to his final resting place: "Have those famed in battle construct a burial-mound, bright after the pyre . . . which shall tower high . . . as a memorial to my people, so that afterwards seafarers will call it Beowulf's Barrow, as they drive from afar their tall ships over the mists of the seas."

Indeed, burial mounds of earth and/or stones (also referred to as barrows, tumuli, and kurgans) have been adopted by numerous cultures throughout time and in much of the world. For example, in England, barrows were employed from the Neolithic Period (c. 4000 BCE) to the late pre-Christian era (c. 600 CE), and they might contain several members of a family or clan. In Japan, during the Tumulus Period (third to sixth century CE), important leaders were buried in tumuli, and one of the largest was made for the fourth-century emperor Nintoku [1594 feet (485 m) long and 115 feet (35 m) high]. Some Japanese tumuli were keyhole-shaped and surrounded by moats. Mound building was also a central component of several Native American cultures along the Mississippi, Tennessee, and Ohio Rivers from around 1000 BCE to 700 CE.

The American Founding Father Thomas Jefferson wrote of his excavations of an Indian burial mound in Virginia: "[The mound] was of spheroidical form, of about 40 feet diameter at the base, and had been of about twelve feet altitude. . . . I first dug superficially in several parts of it, and came to collections of human bones, at different depths, from six inches to three feet below the surface. These were lying in the utmost confusion, some vertical, some oblique, some horizontal . . . to give the idea of bones emptied promiscuously from a bag or basket, and covered over with earth, without any attention to their order." He conjectured that "in this barrow might have been a thousand skeletons."

See also Natufian Funeral Flowers (c. 11,000 BCE), Coffins (c. 4000 BCE), Ossuaries (c. 1000 BCE), Terra-Cotta Army (c. 210 BCE), Viking Ship Burials (834), Cemeteries (1831)

East terrace of Mount Nemrut in modern-day Turkey at sunrise, showing statues and a tumulus formed by piling gravel on the tomb of King Antiochus I of Commagene.

COFFINS

I N THE FAMOUS AMERICAN COWBOY BALLAD "Cowboy's Lament," a dying cowboy implores, "Get six jolly cowboys to carry my coffin. Get six pretty maidens to bear up my pall. Put bunches of roses all over my coffin, roses to deaden the clods as they fall." The word *coffin* often is used broadly to include any boxlike funerary enclosure to hold the dead; however, at least in North America, the term usually denotes a box with six sides (plus a top and bottom), whereas a *casket* is rectangular with four sides. Traditionally, in the West, a village carpenter often made the coffin from wood, but materials for such enclosures today often include steel, wood, and fiberglass.

Coffin comes from the Greek *kophinos*, meaning "basket." In fact, around 4000 BCE, Sumerians placed their dead in baskets made from twigs. Ancient Egyptians used mummy cases that evolved from wooden boxes to ornately decorated enclosures in the shape of the human body. Sometimes a set of mummy cases were nested inside one another like Russian dolls within dolls. Egyptians also used *sarcophagi*—enclosures carved from stone.

In modern Ghana, *fantasy coffins* have become famous with their designs and shapes illustrating some aspect of the life of the deceased. According to the anthropologist Marleen de Witte, "A cocoa farmer may be buried in a cocoa pod coffin, a successful fisherman in a fish, an international businessman in an aeroplane...."

In the 1800s, various "safety coffins" were invented and patented to decrease concerns about accidental **premature burial**. Some involved pipes that could provide air, along with ropes tied to the hands of the seemingly deceased that might ring a bell above the ground. A safety coffin patented in 1897 involved a ball placed on the corpse's chest. A slight movement would release a spring that caused a flag to be raised above the ground. However, this device was impractical and was sensitive to small movements arising from corpse decomposition.

See also Cremation (c. 20,000 BCE), Burial Mounds (c. 4000 BCE), Funeral Processions (c. 1590), Premature Burial (1844)

The Old Shepherd's Chief Mourner (1837) by English painter Sir Edwin Henry Landseer (1802–1873) shows a dog resting his head on his deceased master's coffin.

HEAVEN

ANNE GRAHAM LOTZ (B. 1948)

"DOES HEAVEN EXIST?" ASKS THE HISTORY professor Gary Smith. "The ancient Babylonians, Egyptians, Greeks, and Romans all depicted a future existence where heroes rested, pharaohs resided, or the righteous picnicked in the **Elysian Fields**. Australian Aborigines, as well as early Polynesians, Peruvians, Mexicans, and Native Americans, all had concepts of an afterlife." Through the millennia, people have gazed upward and imagined that gods reside in the sky.

Heaven sometimes has been considered as both the realm in which God or heavenly beings reside and the place to which the righteous go after death. The American Christian evangelist Anne Lotz suggests that heaven is a physical location: a cubical region that is 1,500 miles (2,414 kilometers) on a side, with a base that is "as large as the area from Canada to Mexico, and from the Atlantic Ocean to Rockies," easily able to accommodate 20 billion residents, each one having a private cube with a 75-acre floor.

In ancient Egypt—around the time of the "Pyramid Texts," c. 2400 BCE—Aaru, or the "Field of Reeds," was an eternal heavenly realm for the dead. The early Hebrews did not emphasize life after death, but during later difficult times of the Babylonian exile, the concept of an afterlife increasingly began to make sense to the Jews—if justice was not apparent on earth, maybe it would be in an afterlife. Several heavens exist for Buddhists, but an individual's stay in heaven is considered temporary, with the eventual goal of reaching a state of enlightenment (Nirvana). Similarly, for Hindus, heaven is not a final goal but rather is temporary and related to the physical body. The Christian biblical tradition relates heaven to the Throne of God, and grace enables believers to ascend to heaven. Islamic descriptions of heaven sometimes include physical wish fulfillment, including the wearing of costly clothes and the enjoyment of wine and fancy banquets, and Islamic texts refer to several levels of heaven. Various Mesoamerican and Polynesian religions also have posited different levels of heaven.

See also The Elysian Fields (c. 850 BCE), Reincarnation (c. 600 BCE), Hell (c. 400 BCE), Xibalba (c. 100 BCE), Angels (380), Bifrost (c. 1220), Summer Land (1845), *The Garden of Death* (1896)

The Assumption of the Virgin by Italian painter Francesco Botticini (1446–1497) depicts three hierarchies and nine orders, or ranks, of angels. In the top tier, closest to Jesus and Mary, are the seraphim, cherubim, and thrones.

THE EPIC OF GILGAMESH

THE EPIC OF GILGAMESH—A THOUSAND YEARS older than *The Iliad* or the Bible—is among humankind's oldest recorded tales of a hero. The original was written in the Sumerian language and recorded in cuneiform characters on clay tablets that date back to around 2000 BCE. The Mesopotamians considered the afterlife to be a pale shadow of earthly life, much like the ancient Jewish Sheol mentioned in the Hebrew Bible.

In *Gilgamesh*, the afterlife is described as "the house whose people sit in darkness; dust is their food and clay their meat. They are clothed like birds with wings for covering; they see no light, they sit in darkness." King Gilgamesh is depressed by this vision of the afterlife and begins his quest for immortality. He journeys to the edge of the world to lands seemingly beyond death. At one point, he arrives at Mount Mashu, which guards the rising and the setting of the sun and "whose flank reaches as far as the Netherworld below." Two large scorpion beings protect the way, and they tell him that no man has ever journeyed this far, but nevertheless, they allow him to pass into "the land of night."

After a long journey running through a tunnel or passageway, Gilgamesh emerges in a sparkling garden of jewels where every tree bears precious gems and stones. In this heavenly realm, Gilgamesh gazes with awe on glistening plants made of carnelian, towering lapis lazuli trees, and bushes made of jewels and coral. The author Stephen Mitchell calls this journey "a symbolic death and rebirth, in which he passes through the darkness of an underworld and emerges into the dazzling, *Arabian Nights*-like garden of the gods." Later in his journey, Gilgamesh comes to another dark place where he must cross the Waters of Death on a boat.

Gilgamesh eventually is given a plant that he can eat to live forever. Alas, a serpent steals and consumes the plant, and Gilgamesh remains mortal. One can't help but see parallels between this unfortunate incident and the temptation of Adam and Eve in the Hebrew Bible, in which a serpent seduces them into eating fruit from the forbidden tree of knowledge, thus prompting their expulsion from paradise.

See also *The Egyptian Book of the Dead* (c. 1550 BCE), *The Tibetan Book of the Dead* (c. 780), *The Garden of Death* (1896), Transhumanism (1957)

The **"Burney Relief"** (c. 1800 BCE) is a Mesopotamian terra-cotta depiction of a goddesslike figure— probably Ishtar. In his epic poem, Gilgamesh kills the Bull of Heaven that Ishtar sent to punish him for rejecting her advances.

CAPITAL PUNISHMENT

HAMMURABI (1792–1750 BCE), MOSHEH BEN MAIMON (MAIMONIDES) (1135–1204),
CESARE, MARQUIS OF BECCARIA-BONESANA (1738–1794)

"SOME OF TODAY'S GREATEST MORAL AND legal questions concern capital punishment," writes author Alan Marzilli. "Should the government have the power to sentence convicted criminals to death?" Capital punishment has been sanctioned by most major religions, and Christians and Jews sometimes have justified it with the biblical passage "Whosoever sheddeth a man's blood, by man shall his blood be shed" (Genesis 9:6). Note, however, that civilizations have condoned capital punishment for crimes that range far from loss of life, including blasphemy, adultery, rape, treason, drug trafficking, stealing grapes, and killing chickens. According to the Koran, the death penalty is condoned for robbery, adultery, and apostasy (the renunciation of Islam by a follower). For Jews, the Torah accepts the death penalty for murder, kidnapping, magic, violation of the Sabbath, and various sex crimes.

Through history, some worried that capital punishment was cruel and ineffective. For example, in *On Crimes and Punishments* (1764), Italian jurist and politician Cesare Beccaria famously condemned the death penalty and the torture that often accompanied it. The Jewish scholar Maimonides suggested, "It is better and more satisfactory to acquit a thousand guilty persons than to put a single innocent one to death."

In more recent years, various killing devices have been said to be more humane than methods such as hanging; these devices include the guillotine, the electric chair, the gas chamber, and lethal injection. Since around World War II there has been a trend toward eliminating the death penalty by many governments.

The Babylonian Code of Hammurabi, dating back to about 1772 BCE, recommends the death penalty for twenty-five different crimes (e.g., adultery), although serious crimes such as murder and treason are curiously omitted. Since Hammurabi, the methods of execution have been varied and extreme, including stoning, crucifixion, burning alive, and being "drawn and quartered": having limbs and torso severed, sometimes by being pulled apart by horses tied to one's limbs. In ancient Rome, the crime of parricide—murdering one's parents—was punishable by placing the perpetrator in a sack underwater, along with a live dog, cock, viper, and ape.

See also Guillotine (1792), Crucifixion Vision of Tissot (c. 1890), Electric Chair (1890), Genocide (1944), Death Squads (1980)

This wall mural from St. Venantius Church in Germany depicts the lions employed for the punishment of Venantius of Camerino around 251 CE. According to Christian tradition, Venantius was a teenage martyr during the reign of Roman emperor Trajan Decius.

GRAVESTONES

GRAVE HEADSTONES, ALSO KNOWN AS TOMB-stones and gravestones, are so varied that this entry can focus on only a small portion of their history. For example, such markers are traditional for burials in Muslim, Jewish, and Christian religions and often contain identifying information such as the name of the buried person, along with the date of birth and death.

Stelae and other stone slabs occasionally were used as tombstones in Grecian lands as early as the Mycenaean period (c. 1600– c. 1100 BCE). Later in history, the direction in which headstones pointed was of some concern. For example, in colonial Spanish cemeteries, as in many cemeteries in Europe and North America, gravestones faced east toward the rising sun so that the interred bodies would be ready for the coming Judgment Day. For Muslims, the grave is aligned perpendicular to the Qibla (i.e., the direction to Mecca), and the deceased is placed in the grave with no casket, lying on the right side to face the Qibla. Islamic grave markers are often simple and small relative to those of other religions.

By the middle of the 1600s, cemetery art of colonial New England became rather elaborate, featuring such spooky shapes as a winged death's-head. Some of those headstones also had small openings near the top that represented portals to the afterlife.

Through time, various gravestones have featured inscriptions. For example, we find on Shakespeare's headstone (rendered in modern English): "Blessed be the man that spares these stones, and cursed be he that moves my bones." Today, cemeteries in the United States have become somewhat starker compared with the previous century or two. Stanford Professor Keith Eggener notes, "If you look at grave markers in the 19th-century cemeteries, you'll see the weeping angels, the weeping willows, little sleeping children sitting on top of headstones. These all suggest that death is a kind of presence; it's a gentle sleep. Graves are set up as beds or houses. It's the last house."

See also: Cremation (c. 20,000 BCE), Coffins (c. 4000 BCE), Epitaphs (c. 480 BCE), Grim Reaper (1424), Funeral Processions (c. 1590), Gravediggers (1651), Cemeteries (1831),

A Jewish gravestone in Otwock, Poland, displays a *tzedakah* ("charity") box.

THE EGYPTIAN BOOK OF THE DEAD

"IF YOU'VE EVER WISHED THAT THERE WAS A guidebook to get you into heaven, no matter what your exploits in this life, you're not alone," writes Laura Allsop. "In fact, so strong was the desire for eternal life for the ancient Egyptians that they took things a step further, in the shape of a collection of spells, known as the Book of the Dead, designed to fast-track them through the underworld into paradise."

The Egyptian Book of the Dead is an ancient text that was used in Egypt from around 1550 BCE (or possibly earlier) to 50 BCE. Interestingly, no single *Book of the Dead* exists, and the various papyri contain a varying collection of magical and religious material. Usually, *The Egyptian Book of the Dead* was written in hieroglyphics or hieratic (cursive) script and accompanied by illustrations of a journey into the afterlife. For example, one of the most famous illustrations depicts the heart of the deceased being weighed on the scale of Maat, the goddess of truth and justice. If the heart has the weight of a feather, the deceased may pass into the afterlife. If not, the deceased is devoured by Ammit, a female demon with a body that is part lion, part hippopotamus, and part crocodile.

The Egyptian Book of the Dead usually was placed in the coffin or burial chamber of the dead. Today, we know of around 192 spells that are contained within the book. One spell ensured that the dead would remember their names. Others helped pacify dangerous creatures along the path to the afterlife. Initially, spells in the book were reserved for the royal family, but over time, their use spread to the lower classes.

According to Egyptologist Miriam Lichtheim, "No other nation of the ancient world made so determined an effort to vanquish death and win eternal life.... Eternal life had come to be conceived in the most grandiose terms: the dead were to become godlike and join the company of the gods."

See also Mummies (c. 5050 BCE), *The Epic of Gilgamesh* (c. 2000 BCE), *The Tibetan Book of the Dead* (c. 780)

The ancient Egyptian ritual of "opening of the mouth" described in *The Egyptian Book of the Dead* is performed so that the deceased can eat and drink in the afterlife. In this c. 1300 BCE papyrus, the jackal-headed god Anubis is shown supporting the mummy of the scribe Hunefer while three priests carry out the ritual.

YAMA

ALTHOUGH THERE ARE A NUMBER OF GODS OF death in eastern Asia, among the most widely employed is Yama, who is mentioned in the Hindu Vedic texts that originated in ancient India. The legend of Yama also influenced Buddhism and eventually spread widely in Asia, taking a number of forms in Buddhist, Chinese, Korean, Tibetan, and Japanese mythology.

According to some aspects of Vedic tradition, Yama was the first mortal to have died. For example, in the Rigveda collection of Sanskrit hymns (composed roughly around 1100 BCE), Yama is the first being to travel to the afterlife realm. He is assisted by Chitragupta, the Hindu god who keeps an account of people's earthly behaviors and subsequently helps determine whether they should be reincarnated as a superior or an inferior creature. In Hinduism, Yama has two four-eyed dogs that serve as his guards. This fearsome god Yama often is depicted with blue skin, riding a water buffalo and using a loop or rope to pull souls from corpses. Yama is lord of Naraka, a temporary **hell** or purgatory in which the soul can be purified and from which souls may be redirected to other realms, such as the temporary heaven (*Swarga*), earth, or one of several hells. In the *Abhidharma-kosa*, an important text that is respected and used by schools of Mahayana Buddhism, Yama dwells in the hungry ghost realm (*preta-loka*) below the earthly human world.

Many cultures and religions have had a range of death deities, or lords of death. For example, the ancient Egyptians had Osiris, a god of the afterlife and the underworld. The Greeks had **Hades** and **Thanatos**. The Mesopotamians had Ereshkigal, goddess of the land of the dead. The Aztecs had Mictlantecuhtli. Barastyr was the ruler of the underworld in the mythology of the Ossetian people of the Caucasus region, and Mot was the god of death for the Canaanites. In Norse mythology, Hel is a goddess who presides over the underworld.

See also Hades (c. 850 BCE), Thanatos (c. 700 BCE), Hell (c. 400 BCE), Xibalba (c. 100 BCE), Grim Reaper (1424), Schwabe's *The Death of the Gravedigger* (1895)

Yamantaka, the Destroyer of the God of Death, a Tibetan painting on cloth from the early eighteenth century. If you look closely, you can see that Yamantaka is encircled by three depictions of Yama at the top and two at the bottom, each in a different color.

THE WITCH OF ENDOR

SAUL (C. 1079–C. 1007 BCE)

ACCORDING TO AUTHOR CHRISTIAN DAY, "Many of the great witches of history, folklore, legend, and literature worked with the dead. These fearsome figures have become part of cultural traditions worldwide, inspiring both honor and fear. . . . Perhaps no conjurer of spirits is more famous than the Witch of Endor, a woman who practiced her arts in spite of the condemnation of her ways by the authorities of her time."

In the First Book of Samuel of the ancient Hebrew Scriptures, Saul, the first king of the united kingdom of Israel and Judah, had banned the practice of **necromancy** (communication with the dead). Despite such condemnation and concerned about his impending battle with the Philistines, Saul asks the Witch of Endor to summon the spirit of the prophet Samuel, who appears and asks, "Why have you disturbed me and brought me up?" (1 Samuel 28:15). The deceased prophet goes on to tell Saul that "tomorrow you and your sons will be with me." The sympathetic witch provides food to Saul, who later commits **suicide** as his army is defeated.

Over the centuries, much debate has ensued, with some scholars suggesting that the ghost of Samuel may have been a demon taking his form or an illusion created by the witch. Note that Samuel's phrase "brought me up" implies that the Hebrew abode in the afterlife (called Sheol) is subterranean. Also, his warning that "you and your sons will be with me" suggests that all of the dead—righteous and unrighteous—reside in this underworld, which is often translated in the Bible as **"Hades,"** the ancient Greek realm of the dead.

T. J. Way, an assistant professor of religious studies, notes that "the story of the Witch of Endor—and her dramatic encounter with King Saul—is a little-known biblical tale about fear, hopelessness, and desperation; but it is also a story of mercy, compassion, and great courage. Many contemporary readers are surprised to find a story about a witch in the pages of the Bible."

See also Hades (c. 850 BCE), Necromancy (c. 850 BCE), Suicide (c. 300 BCE), Ghosts (c. 100 CE), Séance (1848)

The Shade of Samuel Invoked by Saul (1857) by Russian artist Dmitri Martynov (1826–1889).

OSSUARIES

c. 1000 BCE

"WE BONES THAT ARE HERE, FOR YOUR BONES we wait." This translation of a meditation and warning appears at the entrance to the Chapel of Bones in Portugal, an ossuary that chillingly features the skulls and other bones of approximately 5,000 monks. Similarly, a plaque at Our Lady of the Conception of the Capuchins in Rome reads in three languages, "What you are now, we once were; what we are now, you shall be." The ossuary at this location features the bones of 4,000 friars. Both of these haunting bone displays suggest the transitory of nature of life and are memento mori works: artistic and symbolic reminders of the inevitability of death and decay.

The term *ossuary* often is used for chests or rooms that house human skeletal remains. Usually, bodies are buried elsewhere to allow several years of bodily decomposition before the bones are transferred to the ossuary. Sometimes ossuaries were created simply as a means to address the overcrowding of cemeteries, making room for the recently deceased. Many of the most fantastically artistic and famous ossuaries are in Europe,

such as the Sedlec Ossuary in the Czech Republic, which features the skeletons of around 50,000 people, some of whose bones have been arranged to form decorations, including a huge chandelier of bones that is said to contain at least one of every bone in the human body. The Douaumont Ossuary in France contains the remains of more than 130,000 French and German soldiers who died in World War I.

During the time of the Second Temple in Jerusalem (516 BCE–70 CE), Jewish burial customs included primary burials in caves, followed by secondary burials in stone ossuary chests placed in niches in the caves. In Persia, the Zoroastrians deposited bones into an *astodan* pit at the center of a raised structure after bodies were exposed to the air and scavenging birds. The earliest Zoroastrian-era ossuaries discovered in Central Asia date back to at least 1000 BCE.

See also Cremation (c. 20,000 BCE), Burial Mounds (c. 4000 BCE), Coffins (c. 4000 BCE), Sky Burial (1328), Thanatourism (1996)

The Sedlec Ossuary in the Czech Republic is estimated to hold the skeletons of 40,000 to 70,000 people. In 1870, woodcarver František Rint created the various bone arrangements—including four chandeliers and a coat of arms—producing a singularly macabre spectacle.

HADES

HERODOTUS (C. 484–425 BCE), ARISTOPHANES (C. 446–C. 386 BCE)

MOST OF OUR UNDERSTANDING OF HADES, the gloomy subterranean realm of the dead in ancient Greek mythology, comes to us from Greek literature, such as Homer's *The Iliad* and *The Odyssey* (c. 850 BCE, according to the Greek historian Herodotus) and Aristophanes's *The Frogs* (405 BCE). Such artistic works not only reflected prevailing images of Hades but probably also helped shape them. Of course, ancient Greek communities probably held quite different beliefs about the afterlife, as there was no centralized religious authority.

For the Greeks, the deceased entered Hades by crossing the Acheron and Styx rivers with the aid of Charon (the ferryman of Hades) and his boat. Charon required a small coin as payment, which relatives usually placed in the mouth of the deceased. The far side of the rivers was guarded by **Cerberus**, the three-headed watchdog of the underworld. Both good and bad people went to Hades, and once they entered the underworld, people appeared to be in a time warp in which they remained at the same age and condition in which they entered the underworld. In Homer's *The Odyssey*, Achilles sums up the dreary existence in Hades when he says he would rather work as a day laborer for a man who had little property than be the lord of all the spirits of the dead.

In several places in the New Testament, the word *Hades* refers to the abode of the dead, with only one passage describing it as a place of torment (see **The Witch of Endor**). For the Greeks, deep in the bowels of Hades was the abyss of Tartarus, where those who had outraged the gods were cast (see **Hell**).

Hades was also the name of the Greek god of the underworld. According to the literature, only a few individuals have managed to leave Hades or its vicinity—including Hercules (who carried Cerberus to the world of the living), Persephone (Hades's wife, who periodically left and returned to Hades, thus creating the four seasons), Orpheus (who charmed Hades with his music), and King Sisyphus (who claimed he needed to return to the living for a proper funeral).

See also Yama (c. 1100 BCE), The Witch of Endor (c. 1007 BCE), The Elysian Fields (c. 850 BCE), Thanatos (c. 700 BCE), Cerberus (c. 560 BCE), Hell (c. 400 BCE), Xibalba (c. 100 BCE), Ondine's Curse (1962)

This fresco by Italian painter Luca Giordano (1632–1705) depicts Charon, the ferryman of Hades, carrying souls of the newly deceased across the rivers of the underworld. **Cerberus**, the three-headed watchdog of Hades, also is shown.

THE ELYSIAN FIELDS

PINDAR (C. 522-443 BCE), PUBLIUS VERGILIUS MARO, OR VIRGIL (70-19 BCE),
LUCIUS MESTRIUS PLUTARCHUS, OR PLUTARCH (C. 46-120 CE)

THE GEOGRAPHY OF THE ANCIENT GREEK afterlife seemed to vary through time and from author to author, but according to some accounts, the Elysian Fields—also called Elysium—was a comfortable section of **Hades** in which those chosen by the gods and/or the righteous would reside in the afterlife. According to the Greek poet Homer, the Elysian Fields was a place of happiness at the end of the earth, on the banks of the Oceanus (or Okeanos), which was thought to be an enormous river encircling the world. In Homer's *The Odyssey* (c. 850 BCE), Elysium is a plain "where life is easiest for men. No snow is there, nor heavy storm, nor ever rain, but ever does the Ocean send up blasts of the shrill-blowing West Wind that they may give cooling to men."

The Greek poet Hesiod (c. 700 BCE) refers to "Isles of the Blessed" inhabited by "happy heroes for whom the grain-giving earth bears honey-sweet fruit flourishing thrice a year, far from the deathless gods." Pindar, a Greek poet who lived around 500 BCE, describes an area where "the good receive a life free from toil, not scraping with the strength of their arms the earth, nor the water of the sea, for the sake of a poor sustenance." For Pindar, the "ocean breezes blow around the island of the blessed, and flowers of gold are blazing, some from splendid trees on land, while water nurtures others." The Roman poet Virgil describes Elysium in *The Aeneid* as including groves, mossy beds, shining fields, and "crystal streams that murmur through the meads."

Finally, Greek historian Plutarch wrote in the first century of the Isles of the Blessed "ten thousand furlongs [1,250 miles] distance from the [African] sea-coast" with winds that "are soft and precipitate dews." The soil is rich and produces "a natural fruit that is plentiful and wholesome enough to feed . . . a leisured folk. . . . Here is the Elysian Field and the abode of the blessed, of which Homer sang."

See also Heaven (c. 2400 BCE), Hades (c. 850 BCE), Bifrost (c. 1220), Summer Land (1845)

Elysian Fields (1903) by German Symbolist painter Carlos Schwabe (1866–1926).

NECROMANCY

PUBLIUS VERGILIUS MARO, OR VIRGIL (70–19 BCE), JOHN DEE (1527–C. 1609), JOHN NAPIER (1550–1617), SYLVIA BROWNE (1936–2013), THERESA CAPUTO (B. 1966), JOHN EDWARD (B. 1969)

IF THERE WERE A WAY TO PREDICT THE MOMENT OF your death, would you choose to know? The practice of foretelling the future or gaining secret knowledge is called divination. Ancient and modern civilizations have explored divination by using an incredible assortment of techniques—from dreams to drugs, from patterns in the stars to messages in the Magic 8 Ball (a children's toy with admittedly limited fortune-telling potential).

Necromancy employs spirits of the dead (sometimes with their bodies) to reveal the future and answer questions. The practice has been associated with ancient Babylonian, Persian, Greek, Roman, and Norse legends, among others. For example, Norse Eddic poems describe stories in which the god Odin (aka "Yule father") has the power to resurrect the dead, and scholars have connected the pagan religious festival of Yule to the Great Hunt, in which the dead were believed to return from their graves and journey, in a procession led by Odin, across the sky. Necromancers—who included such prominent mathematicians as John Dee and John Napier—flourished in the Middle Ages but were condemned by the Catholic Church as "agents of evil spirits." In England, necromancy was outlawed by the Witchcraft Act of 1604.

Among the oldest literary accounts of necromancy is the one found in Homer's *The Odyssey* (c. 850 BCE) and Virgil's Latin epic poem *The Aeneid* (c. 20 BCE), in which Odysseus and Aeneas, respectively, take great risks to journey to the underworld to seek advice from the spirits of people they once knew. In the Hebrew Scriptures, King Saul seeks the necromancy skills of **The Witch of Endor** and asks her to summon the spirit of the prophet Samuel so that Saul can ask about an impending battle. The fifteenth-century *Munich Manual of Demonic Magic* describes how necromancers of yore sometimes stood within protective magic circles in graveyards and used biblical verses and animal sacrifice as part of their rituals. In modern times, demonstrations that verge on necromancy by self-proclaimed mediums such as John Edward, Sylvia Browne, and Theresa Caputo (aka the "Long Island Medium") often are televised.

See also The Witch of Endor (c. 1007 BCE), Cerberus (c. 560 BCE), Sin-Eaters (1825), Séance (1848), *The Grass Harp* (1951), Electronic Voice Phenomena (1956)

C. 850 BCE

The Ghost of Barbara Radziwiłł (1886) by Polish painter Wojciech Gerson (1831–1901). According to legend, King Sigismund Augustus of Poland (1520–1572) asked a renowned sorcerer to evoke the ghost of his beloved wife, Barbara, after her untimely death.

THANATOS

SIGMUND FREUD (1856-1939)

THE WINGED THANATOS WAS ONE OF THE ancient Greek personifications of death and the god who escorted the dead and dying to the underworld. We learn of Thanatos's genealogy from the Greek poet Hesiod, who wrote in his poem *Theogony* (c. 700 BCE) that Thanatos is a son of Nyx, the Greek goddess of the Night, and Erebos, the god of the Darkness. Thanatos had a twin brother named Hypnos, the personification of sleep. Hesiod writes of the brothers: "And there the children of dark Night have their dwellings, Sleep and Death, awful gods. The glowing Sun never looks upon them with his beams. . . . Sleep roams peacefully over the earth and the sea's broad back and is kindly to men; but [Death] has a heart of iron, and his spirit within him is pitiless as bronze: whomsoever of men he has once seized he holds fast: and he is hateful even to the deathless gods."

Homer, in *The Iliad*, presents the famous scene of Thanatos and his brother Hypnos bearing away the body of King Sarpedon, who died a heroic death in battle. Here Thanatos is depicted with a gentler disposition. In ancient Rome, Thanatos also is represented as a more gentle god, and Roman sarcophagi sometimes depict him as a winged boy holding an upside-down torch that represents the extinguishing of life.

Various terms have been derived from Thanatos. During and after the time of Sigmund Freud, the phrase *Thanatos instinct* came to be used to describe the "death drive" that sometimes seems to compel humans to engage in self-destructive behaviors. *Thanatophobia* is an excessive fear of graveyards, corpses, and related items of death. *Thanatology* is the academic study of death. *Thanatosis*, or feigning death, occurs in the animal world as an adaptive behavior for survival. For example, certain insects become still to discourage predators that may be attracted to movement and struggling. When threatened, both the hog-nosed snake and the Virginia opossum may remain motionless while emitting a foul-smelling liquid.

See also Yama (c. 1100 BCE), Hades (c. 850 BCE), Xibalba (c. 100 BCE), Thanatourism (1996)

Thanatos, **a relief** by German sculptor Johann Gottfried Schadow (1764-1850).

REINCARNATION

IAN PRETYMAN STEVENSON (1918–2007)

AY AND NIGHT. LOW TIDE AND HIGH TIDE. THE periodic orbits of planets. Even though our consciousnesses may seem to terminate upon biological death, perhaps it is understandable that some of our ancient ancestors decided that our lives might be cyclical in a process of reincarnation in which human spirits or souls begin new lives in new bodies after biological death.

Most forms of Christianity, Judaism, and Islam tend to have a more linear view of individual lives, but cycles of reincarnation are widely accepted in the major Eastern religions, such as Hinduism, Buddhism, Jainism, and Sikhism. We know that some early beliefs in reincarnation (also referred to as *metempsychosis* and *transmigration*) date to the Iron Age (c. 600 BCE and even earlier) in places such as India and Greece. In Hinduism, *samsara* is the repeating cycle of death and rebirth, and the ultimate goal of life is to escape this process, achieving liberation (*moksha*). Similarly, Buddhists seek to free themselves from all desires and escape *samsara* to attain nirvana. In the ancient Greek world, around the sixth or seventh century BCE, adherents of the religious beliefs of Orphism also believed in reincarnation, and the Pythagoreans (originating in the fifth century BCE) were vegetarians because they believed that souls could reincarnate in the bodies of humans and other animals. Reincarnation was also part of Celtic Druid beliefs and Norse mythology, and it is currently accepted in various African, Native American, and Australian Aboriginal traditions.

Dr. Ian Stevenson is a modern-day psychiatrist who studied the possibility of reincarnation by interviewing more than 2,500 young children who had unusual phobias or apparent memories of previous lives. Researchers continue to debate the degree to which coincidences or experimental deficiencies can affect the results of such fascinating but challenging studies.

See also Heaven (c. 2400 BCE), Hell (c. 400 BCE), *The Tibetan Book of the Dead* (c. 780), *Jacob's Dream* (c. 1805), Near-Death Experiences (1975), Quantum Resurrection (>100 Trillion)

This great "wheel of reincarnation," carved between 1177 and 1249 into China's Mount Baoding, is approximately 25 feet (7.6 meters) tall. The demon Mara, personifying temptation and death, grasps the wheel in his mouth.

CERBERVS

EBJ 1879

CERBERUS

PUBLIUS VERGILIUS MARO, OR VIRGIL (70–19 BCE)
PUBLIUS OVIDIUS NASO, OR OVID (43 BCE–C. 17 CE),

"THERE IS A CAVERN YAWNING DARK AND DEEP, where Hercules dragged the hell-hound Cerberus, fast on a chain, struggling, blinking, screwing up his eyes against the sunlight and the blinding day. . . . Cerberus's three throats filled the air with triple barking, barks of frenzied rage, and spattered the green meadows with white spume." These scary descriptions of the three-headed watchdog of the underworld appear in *Metamorphoses* (8 CE) by the Roman poet Ovid. Once the creature's spittle touched the ground, the liquid turned into poisonous plants.

Cerberus resided on the banks of the subterranean River Styx and appears in both ancient Greek and Roman mythology. This fearsome animal, whose task is to prevent individuals from escaping from **Hades,** is the offspring of the monsters Typhon and Echidna, the latter of which was half woman and half serpent. According to different sources, Cerberus's three heads may represent past, present, and future or birth, youth, and old age. Although it was unimaginably dangerous, the hero Hercules was able to subdue the subterranean Cerberus and carry the beast to the surface. In *The Aeneid*, Virgil's Latin epic poem written around 20 BCE, Cerberus was induced to sleep after eating drugged honey cakes. The legendary musician Orpheus was able to lull the beast to sleep with his music when attempting to rescue his beloved dead wife, Eurydice. Alas, Orpheus forgets his promise not to look back at Eurydice before they both exit Hades, and she vanishes forever, dying a double death.

Cerberus often is depicted with a serpent's tail, although an imaginative rendering on a c. 560 BCE vase from Laconia in southeastern Greece illustrates Cerberus with rows of serpents covering his body and heads.

See also Hades (c. 850 BCE)

The Story of Orpheus: Cerberus (1875) by British artist Edward Burne-Jones (1833–1898).

"THAT'S ALL FOLKS"
MEL BLANC
MAN OF 1000 VOICES
BELOVED HUSBAND AND FATHER
1908 — 1989

EPITAPHS

SIMONIDES OF CEOS (C. 556–468 BCE), LUDOLPH VAN CEULEN (1540–1610),
WILLIAM SHAKESPEARE (1564–1616), KARL HEINRICH MARX (1818–1883),
DAVID HILBERT (1862–1943), WINSTON LEONARD SPENCER-CHURCHILL (1874–1965),
MELVIN JEROME "MEL" BLANC (1908–1989), PAUL ERDÖS (1913–1996),
FRANCIS ALBERT SINATRA (1915–1998)

"EPITAPHS, EMBELLISHMENTS, AND INSCRIPTIONS on churchyard memorials record the frailty of human life—and its continuity," writes author Geoffrey Wright. "They tell us how previous generations lived, and what they believed; they are mirrors of the contemporary social scene."

Epitaphs are short texts honoring the deceased, usually inscribed on their tombstones or commemorative plaques. The custom of identifying the deceased became prominent in ancient Egypt. One of the most famous ancient Greek epitaphs, composed by the poet Simonides of Ceos, records the burial location of the fallen Spartans at the battle of Thermopylae (480 BCE): "O Stranger, send the news home to the people of Sparta that here we are laid to rest: the commands they gave us have been obeyed."

Many epitaphs are brief records consisting simply of the deceased's name and years of birth and death. However, many famous epitaphs have been more elaborate. As mentioned in the entry on **gravestones**, William Shakespeare's epitaph reads (in modern spelling): "Blessed be the man that spares these stones, and cursed be he that moves my bones." Sir Winston Churchill's epitaph: "I am ready to meet my Maker. Whether my Maker is prepared for the great ordeal of meeting me is another matter." Karl Marx: "The philosophers have only interpreted the world in various ways; the point however is to change it." Comedian Mel Blanc: "That's all folks." Frank Sinatra: "The best is yet to come." As for three famous mathematicians, David Hilbert had (in English): "We must know. We will know." Paul Erdös: "I've finally stopped getting dumber." Ludolph van Ceulen: "3.141592653589793238 46264338327950288."

"Death stalks us from the moment we are born," writes author Kathleen Miller, "and we all know that someday, somehow, we will have to confront our own mortality. In this final feud, why shouldn't we have the last word? Hence: the epitaph."

See also Gravestones (c. 1600 BCE), Obituaries (1731), Death Certificate (1770), Death Mask (c. 1888), Last Words of the Dying (1922)

Headstone of comedian and voice actor Mel Blanc at the Hollywood Forever Cemetery in southern California. "That's all folks" was a phrase used by one of Blanc's characters, Porky Pig.

HELL

DURANTE DEGLI ALIGHIERI (C. 1265–1321),
CHARLES GRANDISON FINNEY (1792–1875)

N HIS FOURTEENTH-CENTURY EPIC POEM *INFERNO*, Italian poet Durante degli Alighieri (commonly known as Dante) enters the gate of hell and sees the inscription "Abandon all hope, ye who enter here." In 1831, revivalist preacher Charles G. Finney shouted about hell, "Look! Look! See the millions of wretches, biting and gnashing their tongues, as they lift their scalding heads from the burning lake!"

Despite these frightening images, when the concept of hell got its start, it was not the place of eternal torture and punishment for the wicked; rather, it was simply an "underworld" for the wandering souls of the dead. "This kind of neutral underworld," write authors Chuck Crisafulli and Kyra Thompson, "spanned cultures and centuries, from the Mesopotamians to the ancient Chinese to the Aztecs." Early Israelites and Greeks believed in the subterranean Sheol and **Hades**, respectively, in which both good and evil souls resided, but these underworlds do not typically refer to a place of eternal torture or punishment. "In Eastern religions," write Crisafulli and Thompson, "belief in **reincarnation** meant that hell, rather than being a place of eternal torment, was more

akin to a horrible temp job: You put in your time burning off the ugly sins of one life and get ready for another go at living a good life."

The ancient Greeks did have their Tartarus, a specific deep pit of torment for the wicked within Hades, described by Plato in *Gorgias* (c. 400 BCE). The Koran describes a fiery Islamic hell of many different levels, and the ancient Chinese believed in a version of hell referred to as Diyu, an underground maze of chambers where souls atone for their sins.

The New Testament mentions Hades and Gehenna. Here, Gehenna is a place of everlasting torment, and it appears to refer to the Valley of Hinnom, in which children were sacrificed to the Canaanite god Moloch. The Romans later used the area as a garbage pit and cremation site where fire burned almost continuously, and this may have led to the fiery metaphor for hell.

See also Heaven (c. 2400 BCE), The Witch of Endor (c. 1007 BCE), Hades (c. 850 BCE), Reincarnation (c. 600 BCE), Xibalba (c. 100 BCE), Outer Darkness (c. 80 CE), Dante's *The Divine Comedy* (1321), Golding's Liminal World (1956)

C. 400 BCE

Medieval image of hell in the *Hortus deliciarum* (c. 1180), compiled by the nun Herrad of Landsberg (c. 1130–1195). This illuminated encyclopedia was intended for use by young novices at the Hohenburg Abbey in Alsace, France.

SUICIDE

LOUIS XIV (1638-1715), YUKIO MISHIMA (1925-1970)

ON NOVEMBER 25, 1970, YUKIO MISHIMA (PEN name Kimitake Hiraoka), one of the most important Japanese authors of the twentieth century, nominated three times for the Nobel Prize in Literature, plunged a knife into his abdomen, slicing it open in the Japanese ritual suicide by disembowelment. His act of *seppuku*, traditionally undertaken by samurai warriors after a loss of honor, took place after an unsuccessful attempt to restore the power of the emperor.

Throughout history, individuals have attempted to bring about their own deaths via hanging, pesticide poisoning, firearms, and other methods. The causes of such acts include despair, mental illness, social protest, and—as exemplified by modern-day suicide bombers and Japanese **kamikaze pilots** who deliberately crashed planes into American targets—terrorist or military tactics. In India, historical accounts dating as far back as the fourth century BCE describe the practice of *sati*, in which widows immolate themselves on their deceased husbands' funeral pyres. Around 73 CE, 960 members of the Jewish community at Masada, Israel, killed themselves rather than be conquered and enslaved by the Romans, and in 1978, a comparable number of American religious "cult" followers committed mass suicide by cyanide in Jonestown, a settlement in Guyana.

According to the World Health Organization, suicide is currently the second leading cause of death in 15- to 29-year-olds worldwide, with the highest rates of suicide occurring in Eastern Europe and Asia. Judaism, Christianity, and Islam traditionally considered suicide an offense against God, and various countries have attempted to outlaw suicide and suicide attempts. In 1670, Louis XIV of France ordered that the corpse of a suicide victim be drawn facedown through the streets and that all of the person's property be confiscated to punish the family.

Today, researchers have found that low levels of brain-derived neurotrophic factor (BDNF) sometimes are associated with suicide. Whatever the biological and psychosocial triggers, historian Jeffery Watt reminds us that "suicide and attitudes toward self-inflicted death offer an invaluable window into the collective mentality of a given society."

See also: Martyr (c. 135), Children and *Capacocha* (1622), *Ophelia* (1852), Euthanasia (1872), Electric Chair (1890), Kamikaze Pilots (1944), Do Not Resuscitate (1976)

The suicide of Dido, the legendary first queen of ancient Carthage, is shown in this 1872 painting by Belgian artist Joseph Stallaert (1825–1903). According to Virgil's *The Aeneid* (19 BCE), she stabs herself atop a pyre as her beloved Aeneas, a Trojan hero, is leaving her kingdom.

TERRA-COTTA ARMY

QIN SHI HUANG (259–210 BCE)

GAZING AT THE UNEARTHED TERRA-COTTA ARMY can give one the feeling of entering a new universe, an underworld in some other dimension in which frozen figures both protect and entertain their dead master for time without end. "For centuries, farmers living in villages east of Xi'an in northwestern China heard stores of ghosts and spirits living beneath the earth," writes author Michael Capek. Finally, the accidental unearthing in 1974 of a terra-cotta (baked clay) soldier by farmers triggered years of archaeological study as well as the discovery of a vast subterranean army guarding a dead emperor for more than 2,000 years.

The life-size terra-cotta figures represent the armies of Qin Shi Huang, the first emperor of China, and they were buried with the emperor around 210 BCE to protect him in his afterlife. Estimates suggest the presence of around 670 horses, 130 chariots, and perhaps more than 8,000 soldiers, most of which are still buried! Many of the soldiers were originally brightly colored and once held actual weapons such as swords, crossbows, and spears. Also present are terra-cotta musicians and acrobats.

Emperor Qin ascended to the throne at age 13, and it is estimated that the construction of his mausoleum started around that time and involved about 700,000 workers. Evidence also suggests that body parts were created in an assembly line–like fashion, using various face molds. Faces subsequently were modified to produce additional variation and individualized expressions.

Qin turned a China of warring states into the core of a single nation. During the feudal period in China, sometimes slaves, soldiers, and women were buried alive in the same tomb with the deceased master so that they could serve his needs in the afterlife. Fortunately, by the time of Qin, this custom no longer was practiced—for him, the terra-cotta people sufficed. According to later writers, the emperor's tomb also contained other wonders, including human-made streambeds flowing with mercury to mimic coursing water. Analysis of nearby soils has indeed revealed a high level of mercury.

See also Mummies (c. 5050 BCE), Burial Mounds (c. 4000 BCE), Golem (1580), Children and *Capacocha* (1622)

A view of the Terra-Cotta Army within excavation pit 1 near Xi'an, China.

XIBALBA

EL CAPITÁN PEDRO DE ALVARADO Y CONTRERAS (C. 1490–1541)

XIBALBA (PRONOUNCED SHE-BAL-BA) IS THE name of the mysterious underworld in the mythology of the K'iche' Maya people—Native Americans mostly from the highlands of present-day Guatemala—who were conquered by the conquistador Pedro de Alvarado in 1524. The subterranean Xibalba ("the place of fright") was accessible by a cave and inhabited by various horrifying death gods described in the Popol Vuh, a set of texts detailing the mythology and history of the K'iche' kingdom. Twelve powerful godlike rulers inhabit Xibalba and cause various forms of human suffering in our world, such as fear, sickness, and pain. The realm of Xibalba is replete with various tests for humans, and even the path to Xibalba has challenges such as separate rivers filled with scorpions, blood, and pus. In one famous legend, twins Hunahpu and Xbalanque enter Xibalba, seeking revenge for the gods' killing of their father and uncle. After the death gods subject the twins to a series of daily ball games and trials, the heroes finally decapitate them and are reborn as heavenly objects in the sky. Depictions that allude to the myth of the hero twins have been found on murals dating to approximately 100 BCE.

The spatial cosmology of the Maya included a universe with many layers—a flat, square earth with a central world tree connecting the thirteen-layered **heaven** to the nine-layered underworld where the Xibalbans lived. Often depicted as diseased creatures, some Xibalbans wear necklaces of eyeballs. Within Xibalba there were several houses associated with different trials and traps, including rooms with sharp knives, jaguars, bats, heat, cold, and more.

According to author Stanislav Chládek, Maya religious thoughts were "permeated with belief in an afterlife, which could take place only after the dead passed through the trials of Xibalba, ruled by the Lords of the Underworld, Xibalbans. Ever-present death led the Maya to dedicate much of their ritual to this final confrontation with the underworld's lords and their own eventual rebirth."

See also Heaven (c. 2400 BCE), Yama (c. 1100 BCE), Hades (c. 850 BCE), Thanatos (c. 700 BCE), Hell (c. 400 BCE), Day of the Dead (1519), Children and *Capacocha* (1622)

This carved limestone relief depicts bound captives (lower left) who are presented to a Maya ruler around 785. Sacrificial bloodletting often was performed on high-status prisoners of war—as opposed to low-status captives, who often were used for labor—during the Classic period of Maya culture (c. 250–900).

udita me deus et dister
ne caulam meam de
gente non sancta ab
homine iniquo et doloso eru

pe me quia tu es deus meus
et fortitudo mea. ps
mitte lucem tuam et
ueritatem tuam ipsa me de

RESURRECTION

"RESURRECTION IS UNQUESTIONABLY ONE OF THE most important and intriguing concepts of the Christian faith," writes religious scholar Geza Vermes. "Saint Paul, to whom this region owes more than to anyone else, leaves his readers in no doubt in this respect." According to Paul (1 Corinthians 15:13–14), "If there is no resurrection of the dead, then not even Christ has been raised. And if Christ has not been raised, our preaching is useless and so is your faith."

The term *resurrection* in a religious context refers to the dead returning to life and still retaining their individuality. Most religious Christians believe that Jesus was resurrected with his material body after he was crucified and placed in a tomb. More generally, the Abrahamic religions postulate a resurrection of the dead at the end of the world. For example, Muslims believe in a future day of bodily resurrection and a final assessment of humanity by Allah. The Hebrew Bible books of Ezekiel and Daniel both suggest that Israelites will rise from the dead in the future.

Several people are resurrected in the Hebrew Bible. The prophet Elijah prays, and God raises a young boy from death. A dead man is resurrected when his body touches Elisha's bones in a tomb. In the New Testament, Jesus authorizes his apostles to raise the dead.

Interestingly, Muslims do not believe that Jesus was crucified but rather that he was raised bodily to heaven by God. The Koran (4:157–158) states, "They said (in boast), 'We killed Christ Jesus . . .' but they killed him not, nor crucified him, but so it was made to appear to them. . . . Nay, Allah raised him up unto Himself." According to Muslims, when Jesus returns at the end of the world, he will "break the cross, kill the pigs, and abolish the jizya tax" (Hâdith Number 656). Since the *jizyah* is the compulsory tax that non-Muslims must pay to live in a Muslim land, one interpretation suggests that Christians will then convert to Islam.

See also Four Horsemen of the Apocalypse (c. 70 CE), Golem (1580), Resurrectionists (1832), Walking Corpse Syndrome (1880), Crucifixion Vision of Tissot (c. 1890), Ghost Dance (1890), Cardiopulmonary Resuscitation (1956), Zombies (1968), Quantum Resurrection (>100 Trillion)

"The Raising of Lazarus," an illustration from the illuminated manuscript *Les Très Riches Heures du duc de Berry* (c. 1412–1416) by the Limbourg brothers.

NATIONAL POLICE GAZETTE.

Vol. 2. No. 27—$2 A YEAR.   NEW-YORK, SATURDAY, MARCH 13, 1847.   FOUR CENTS A NUMBE

THE FEMALE ABORTIONIST.

ABORTION

PEDANIUS DIOSCORIDES (C. 40–90 CE)

THE PRACTICE OF ABORTION STARTED thousands of years ago, when terminations of pregnancy were attempted using a large variety of effective and ineffective means that ranged from herbs and firm abdominal massage to the insertion of sharpened instruments. For example, around 70 CE the Greek pharmacologist Dioscorides suggested use of "abortion wine" made from hellebore, squirting cucumber, and scammony, which are all plants. Soranus, a second-century Greek physician, prescribed riding animals to induce abortion or leaping energetically so that the woman's heels touched her buttocks. Today, the removal or expulsion of an embryo or fetus from the uterus is accomplished by various procedures. For example, *medical abortions* are nonsurgical and make use of certain drugs. *Vacuum aspiration* employs a manual syringe or electric pump. *Dilation and curettage* makes use of a scraping tool.

Abortion is a source of considerable debate, with some suggesting that even the destruction of a fertilized egg is murder of a human being. However, as discussed by the ethicist Louis Guenin, "zygotic personhood" (the idea that a fertilized egg is a person) is a recent concept.

For example, before 1869, the Catholic Church accepted the notion that the embryo was not a person until it was 40 days old, at which time the soul entered. Aristotle also presumed this 40-day threshold for male embryos, with a 90-day threshold for females. If the early embryo was soulless, perhaps early abortion was not murder. Pope Innocent III in 1211 determined that the time of ensoulment corresponded to the moment of "quickening," when movements from the fetus are first felt—anywhere from three to four months. In Jewish law, the fetus becomes a full-fledged human being when its head exits the womb. Before the embryo is 40 days old, it is *maya B'alma*, or "mere water" (Talmud, Yevamot 69b).

In the 1973 case *Roe v. Wade*, the United States Supreme Court invalidated state laws banning abortion, ruling that such laws violated a woman's right to privacy. In particular, the state cannot restrict a woman's right to an abortion in any way during the first trimester (first three months of pregnancy).

See also Suicide (300 BCE), Children and *Capacocha* (1622), Autopsy (1761), Euthanasia (1872), Brain Death (1968), Do Not Resuscitate (1976)

This illustration of New York City abortionist Ann Lonham (a.k.a. Madame Restell, 1812-1878) appears in an 1847 edition of the *National Police Gazette*. She committed suicide at her Fifth Avenue residence shortly after her arrest by Anthony Comstock, founder of the New York Society for the Suppression of Vice.

FOUR HORSEMEN OF THE APOCALYPSE

NERO (37–68 CE), DOMITIAN (51–96 CE), ALBRECHT DÜRER (1471–1528),
BENJAMIN WEST (1738–1820), TERRY PRATCHETT (1948–2015), NEIL GAIMAN (B. 1960)

THE APOCALYPSE OF JOHN, ALSO KNOWN AS THE Book of Revelation, is the final book of the New Testament and has been the subject of much discussion, artwork, literature, and debate because of its frightening content and startling images that are open to a range of interpretations. Revelation probably was composed between 69 and 95 CE, near the end of the reign of Roman emperor Nero or Domitian, depending on the scholar consulted. According to the text itself, the author of Revelation is John from the Greek island of Patmos. Many interpretations exist; for example, the text may be meant to describe various historical events associated with the Roman Empire, future events involving the end times, the struggle between good and evil, and/or the Second Coming of Jesus Christ.

Among the famous and perplexing images in Revelation are the Four Horsemen of the Apocalypse: beings who seem to be summoned and released when Jesus Christ (symbolized by a lamb) opens the first four seals on a scroll. In common interpretations, the first three horsemen—who ride out on white, red, and black horses—represent conquest (or pestilence), war, and famine, respectively. The last horse has a pale color and represents death (Revelation 6:7–8, New International Version): "When the Lamb opened the fourth seal, I heard the voice of the fourth living creature say, 'Come and see!' I looked and there before me was a pale horse! Its rider was named Death, and Hell was following close behind him. They were given power over a fourth of the earth to kill by sword, famine, and plague, and by the wild beasts of the earth."

The Greek word for the actual color of Death's horse (*khloros*) can have several meanings, such as ashen, pale, pale green, and yellowish green. A 1505 charcoal drawing by the German artist Albrecht Dürer shows Death as a skeleton holding a scythe and sitting on a bony horse. In 1796, American painter Benjamin West depicted the Horseman of Death followed by monsters. Terry Pratchett and Neil Gaiman's World Fantasy Award–winning novel *Good Omens* (1990) culminates with the gathering of the "Bikers of the Repocalypse," including the beautiful red-haired War and the boyish Pollution, the latter of whom allegedly took the place of Pestilence after the advent of antibiotics.

See also Resurrection (c. 30 CE), Black Death (1347), Grim Reaper (1424), *The Garden of Death* (1896)

Death on a Pale Horse (1796) by the American painter Benjamin West (1738–1820).

OUTER DARKNESS

HERBERT LOCKYER (1886–1984)

C. 80 CE

TO WHERE DO OUR SUPRALIMINAL SPIRITS drift at the moment of death? According to the Christian New Testament Gospel of Matthew, there may exist a mysterious realm of "outer darkness," which is mentioned three times in this Gospel. Outer darkness seems to refer to a location into which a person may be "cast out" and where there is a "weeping and gnashing of teeth" because the person is separated from God. The religious expert and pastor Dr. Herbert Lockyer writes, "We do not know all that is implied by 'outer darkness,' or the darkness of the outside. We cannot see through the veil and penetrate the darkness, and tell of the sufferings within it. . . . Particulars of the torments of the wicked are not revealed. The only safety from them is to hide in His bosom."

Author and reporter Drew Williams writes on the concept of outer darkness according to the beliefs of Mormons: "Latter-day revelation notes that, having meted out all of the glory and mercy to even the lowliest of souls, God still needed a place for the most wicked of spirits, such as those who chose to follow Satan in defiance of the plan presented at the Grand Council. . . . No spirit of God dwells in [the outer darkness]. Outer Darkness is the ultimate exile." According to Williams, those people who knew Jesus Christ as the Messiah yet denied the truth are condemned souls who "will suffer in eternal darkness and torment forever. These lost souls would rather have never been born."

Pastor J. D. Faust writes, "Some modern Christians hold that this 'outer darkness' is a temporary prison in the heart of the earth where carnal Christians will spend the millennium. . . . Others teach that 'outer darkness' is only a realm above ground *within* the kingdom. . . . Some teach that there is *also* a further possibility of being cast down into the underworld depending on the degree of sin; but they would distinguish this underworld from 'outer darkness.'"

See also Hades (c. 850 BCE), Hell (c. 400 BCE), Dante's *The Divine Comedy* (1321), Golding's Liminal World (1956)

The Ladder of Divine Ascent, a twelfth-century painting at St. Catherine's Monastery at the foot of Mount Sinai in Egypt. The monks are tempted and pulled down by demons, while angels encourage them to continue their ascent to the top of the thirty-rung ladder, where Jesus is waiting for them. At the bottom of the painting, the gaping mouth of the Devil is visible.

GHOSTS

GAIUS PLINIUS CAECILIUS SECUNDUS, OR PLINY THE YOUNGER (61–C. 112)

IN THE 1843 NOVEL *A CHRISTMAS CAROL* BY Charles Dickens, a ghost realizes that Ebenezer Scrooge does not believe in ghosts. The ghost asks, "What evidence would you have of my reality beyond that of your senses? Why do you doubt your senses?" "Because," replies Scrooge, "a little thing affects them. A slight disorder of the stomach makes them cheats. You may be an undigested bit of beef. . . . There's more of gravy than of grave about you, whatever you are!"

Although the idea that the soul or sprit of a dead person can manifest to the living has been around even in preliterate folk religions and appears to have been pervasive throughout cultures, this entry is dated to circa 100 CE, to one of the earliest classic accounts of a haunted house, with a chain-clanking ghost, followed by an investigation. Roman magistrate Pliny the Younger recounted the tale of a house in Athens that was haunted by a ghost bound in chains. After an investigation, the ghost's buried shackled skeleton was discovered and then properly reburied, which caused the haunting to cease.

Through time, ghosts have taken a range of apparent manifestations, from invisible presences to solid, lifelike entities. Ghosts in Homer's *The Iliad* and *The Odyssey* are described as disappearing "as a vapor, gibbering and whining into the earth." Skeptics have suggested that such ghostly visions can result from pareidolia, the human tendency to find familiar patterns in somewhat random perceptions. The visions also can result from hypnagogic hallucinations experienced at the borders of sleep and wakefulness.

"No doubt ghosts do reflect some of our concerns about what happens to us after we die," writes author J. Allan Danelek. "After all, if there are ghosts, then it demonstrates that the human personality does survive death, giving all of us the hope of immortality. As such, even while they frequently terrify us, it seems we need ghosts, if only for our personal sense of cosmic significance."

See also *The Egyptian Book of the Dead* (c. 1550 BCE), *The Witch of Endor* (c. 1007 BCE), Sin-Eaters (1825), Séance (1848)

This illustration by famous Japanese painter and printmaker Utagawa Kuniyoshi (1797–1861) shows an enormous ghost reciting a poem outside the study of the poet Minamoto no Tsunenobu (1016–1097).

MARTYR

AKIVA BEN JOSEPH (C. 50–C. 135), VIBIA PERPETUA (C. 182–203), RALPH WALDO EMERSON (1803–1882), SØREN AABYE KIERKEGAARD (1813–1855), MOHANDAS KARAMCHAND GANDHI (1869–1948), MARTIN LUTHER KING, JR. (1929–1968)

"LET US ALL BE BRAVE ENOUGH TO DIE THE death of a martyr, but let no one lust for martyrdom," said Mahatma Gandhi, the famous nationalist leader in British-ruled India. American poet Ralph Waldo Emerson wrote, "The martyr cannot be dishonored. Every lash inflicted is a tongue of fame; every prison a more illustrious abode." According to Danish philosopher Søren Kierkegaard, "The tyrant dies and his rule is over; the martyr dies and his rule begins."

Originally, the term *martyr* meant "witness," but during the early centuries of Christian history, the word came to imply suffering or death as a result of one's beliefs. Similarly, in Arabic, the word *shaheed* means "witness" and came to be used for Muslim martyrs who died for their faith.

In the second century, Jewish scholar Hananiah ben Teradion became a martyr when the Roman emperor made it illegal to teach and study the Torah. Ben Teradion was arrested, wrapped in a Torah scroll, and placed on a pyre. According to legend, as the fires started, he said, "The parchments burn, but the words fly free." Similarly, the Romans killed Rabbi Akiva ben Joseph around 135 because he taught the Torah. While the Roman legionnaires tore his flesh from his bones with large iron combs, he continued reciting the *Shema*, a Jewish prayer.

In the classic "age of martyrdom" during the Roman persecution of Christians, the death of a martyr was considered a "baptism in blood" that cleansed the martyr of sin. Sainthood frequently was granted to these highly venerated individuals, whose relics proliferated in many Catholic and Orthodox churches. In 203, for example, the 22-year-old Christian noblewoman and nursing mother Vibia Perpetua of Carthage was condemned to death, along with her pregnant slave, Felicitas. Placed in the Roman arena, they were attacked by a wild bull and then executed by sword. Both martyrs were granted sainthood and are commemorated on March 7 by most Christians.

Today, religious martyrdom is widespread, and the concept of political martyrdom has emerged to describe one who suffers or dies for a political belief or cause, as in the case of civil rights activist Martin Luther King, Jr.

See also Suicide (300 BCE), Last Words of the Dying (1922), Kamikaze Pilots (1944)

The Christian Martyrs' Last Prayer (1883) by French painter Jean-Léon Gérôme (1824–1904).

ANGELS

"FOUR CORNERS TO MY BED, FOUR ANGELS round my head. One to watch and one to pray, and two to bear my soul away." This ancient nursery rhyme probably caused some to picture angels with wings lifting them to heaven, but in early historical images, angels often did not have wings. In fact, the earliest known Christian representation of angels with wings is on the "Prince's Sarcophagus" (c. 380) found near Istanbul. In Zoroastrianism, Islam, Judaism, and Christianity, angels often act as intermediaries between heaven and earth.

In the Old and New Testaments, where angels are mentioned nearly 300 times, they are depicted as both helping humans and causing their deaths, as when the Angel of Death slew the firstborn children of the Egyptians in the Book of Exodus. Around 500 CE, the Christian theologian Pseudo-Dionysius developed a hierarchy of nine angelic ranks, ordered by their perceived closeness to God: (1) seraphim, (2) cherubim, (3) thrones, (4) dominions, (5) virtues, (6) powers, (7) principalities, (8) archangels, and finally (9) angels.

First on the list are the seraphim that guard the throne of God and are described in Isaiah 6:1–4 as having six wings. Most of us think of cherubs as chubby little babies flying around on Valentine's Day cards. In the Bible, however, they are much scarier—at the edge of Eden with a flaming sword and ordered to prevent Adam and Eve from returning. According to Ezekiel 1:5–14, they have four faces (human, lion, ox, eagle) and four wings. Jesus spoke of angels in Matthew 26:53: "Do you think I cannot call on my Father, and he will at once put at my disposal more than twelve legions of angels?"

One of the most enigmatic stories in the Bible occurs in Genesis 6:1–4, where we find the Nephilim, who are born when "the sons of God went to the daughters of men and had children by them. They were the heroes of old, men of renown." Some speculate that the "sons of god" were angels who mated with human females to produce hybrid beings known as the Nephilim.

See also Heaven (c. 2400 BCE), *Jacob's Dream* (c. 1805), Schwabe's *The Death of the Gravedigger* (1895), *The Wounded Angel* (1903)

This painting by Danish artist Carl Heinrich Bloch (1834–1890) shows an angel comforting Jesus in the garden of Gethsemane before his arrest and crucifixion.

THE TIBETAN BOOK OF THE DEAD

YESHE TSOGYAL (757–817), CARL GUSTAV JUNG (1875–1961),
WALTER YEELING EVANS-WENTZ (1878–1965), WILLIAM S. BURROUGHS (1914–1997),
IRWIN ALLEN GINSBERG (1926–1997)

IN CONSIDERING *THE TIBETAN BOOK OF THE DEAD*, medical oncologists and professors Mark Bower and Jonathan Waxman write, "A fundamental tenet of Buddhism is that death is not something that awaits us in some distant future, but something that we bring with us into the world and that accompanies us throughout our lives. Rather than a finality, death offers a unique opportunity for spiritual growth with the ultimate prospect of transformation into an immortal state of benefit to others."

The Tibetan Book of the Dead—also known as *Liberation through Hearing* during the Intermediate State, or *Bardo Thodol*—is a Tibetan text that has been used to guide dying people through various experiences during the 49-day interval between death and the next rebirth. This intermediate period is referred to as the *bardo*, and it can be filled with both peaceful and frightening visions. The book is a guide that is read aloud to the dead and dying, and the goal is *not* to be reborn but to be free of the cycle of rebirth and death.

According to Tibetan tradition, the text was composed and/or compiled during the eighth century by the legendary Buddhist mystic Guru Padmasambhava and written down by his consort, Yeshe Tsogyal, c. 780. In 1927, the American anthropologist Walter Evans-Wentz introduced the text to the West.

Because *The Tibetan Book of the Dead* attempts to address one of humanity's greatest questions—What happens to us when we die?—it has attracted interest from diverse groups ranging from musicians such as the Beatles to influential psychiatrists such as Carl Jung. "Beat Generation" author William S. Burroughs wrote to poet Allen Ginsberg in 1954, "Tibetan Buddhism is extremely interesting. Dig it if you have not done so." When Evans-Wentz died in 1965, his translation of *The Tibetan Book of the Dead* was read at his funeral.

See also *The Epic of Gilgamesh* (c. 2000 BCE), *The Egyptian Book of the Dead* (c. 1550 BCE), Yama (c. 1100 BCE), Reincarnation (c. 600 BCE), Sky Burial (1328)

"Dance of the Lord of Death" in a Bhutan festival honoring the legendary Padmasambhava, who is said to have brought Vajrayana Buddhism to Tibet and Bhutan during the eighth century.

VIKING SHIP BURIALS

DAVID HERBERT LAWRENCE (1885–1930)

"AVE YOU BUILT YOUR SHIP OF DEATH, O HAVE you?" asked English author D. H. Lawrence in his haunting poem "The Ship of Death," which describes boats carrying souls on the "longest journey." Lawrence counsels readers to furnish their own ships with food and wine to prepare for the "dark flight" to oblivion. The poet appears to be referring to the mysterious ship burials of the Vikings, in which the deceased were placed in boats along with various possessions and sometimes even with sacrificed slaves.

One of the most famous Viking ships used for burial during the Viking Age is the Oseberg ship discovered in a large burial mound in Norway. In 834, this oak ship, some 70 feet (21 meters) long, was interred along with fourteen horses, an ox, and three dogs, as determined from skeletal remains. Also on board were the skeletons of two women—one who died at about 64 years of age, the other at about 25. It has been speculated that the older woman may have been Åsa, a semilegendary queen who was famous both for her beauty and for ensuring that King Gudrød the Hunter, her cruel husband, was killed. The ship also contained a cart, sleighs, ornaments, and tools.

Another famous example of Viking ship burials is the Gokstad ship (76 feet, or 23 meters, long), found in a Norwegian burial mound. The Gokstad, sturdier than the Oseberg ship, was intended for trade and warfare and could accommodate thirty-two oarsmen. The wood of the ship was dated to around 890. On board was a man of about 60 years of age, and the burial mound also contained three small boats and a peacock, along with many shields, dogs, and horses.

In the tenth century, Ahmad ibn Fadlan—a famous Arab Muslim writer and traveler—wrote of the funeral of a Scandinavian chieftain whose female slave volunteered to join him in the afterlife. After being given intoxicants, she had sex with many of the men, who then placed her at the side of the corpse in the funeral ship and raped her. She then was strangled and stabbed by an old woman called the "Angel of Death," and the ship was set afire.

See also Burial Mounds (c. 4000 BCE), Gravestones (c. 1600 BCE), Bifrost (c. 1220), Sky Burial (1328), Funeral Processions (c. 1590), Cemeteries (1831),

An 1883 painting by Polish painter Henryk Siemiradzki (1843–1902) illustrates a ship burial for a Viking ruler who died in the tenth century.

BIFROST

SNORRI STURLUSON (1179–1241), GEORGE MACDONALD (1824–1905)

I N *THE GOLDEN KEY,* A FAIRY TALE PUBLISHED IN 1867, Scottish minister George MacDonald associates the rainbow with wonder and mystery: "They climbed out of the earth; and, still climbing, rose above it. They were in the rainbow. Far abroad, over ocean and land, they could see through its transparent walls the earth beneath their feet. Stairs beside stairs wound up together, and beautiful beings of all ages climbed along with them. They knew that they were going up to the country whence the shadows fall."

Perhaps the most intriguing association of the rainbow with unearthly realms is Bifrost (roughly pronounced BIV-rost), the burning rainbow bridge that ascends from our world to Asgard, the realm of the gods, in the *Prose Edda,* Norse mythological texts written and compiled around 1220 by the Icelandic historian and poet Snorri Sturluson. The gods built Bifrost from fire (red), air (blue), and water (green), and though the rainbow bridge may look fragile, it is extremely strong.

The gods use Bifrost in their frequent travels to earth, but mortals cannot traverse it—except, perhaps, certain valiant men who are killed in battle. According to the ancient texts, the bridge will be destroyed at Ragnarök, a time in the future of great natural disasters and the death of many of the major gods. At the climax of Ragnarök, giants and demons attack Asgard via Bifrost. Bifrost is guarded by the god Heimdallr, who sounds his Gjallarhorn to alert the gods. Alas, despite Heimdallr's efforts, Bifrost is destroyed under the invaders' weight.

Rainbows have played important roles in legends and religions around the world. For example, in Greco-Roman mythology, the rainbow also served as a path between earth and heaven. Authors Raymond Lee and Alistair Fraser write, "From the Occident to the Orient comes a dizzying array of imagined rainbows. Whether as bridge, messenger, archer's bow, or serpent, the rainbow has been pressed into symbolic services for millennia."

See also Heaven (c. 2400 BCE), Viking Ship Burials (834), *Jacob's Dream* (c. 1805)

The god Heimdallr stands by the Bifrost rainbow bridge, blowing into Gjallarhorn, in this 1905 depiction by German illustrator Emil Doepler (1855–1922).

DANTE'S
THE DIVINE COMEDY

PUBLIUS VERGILIUS MARO (70–19 BCE), DANTE ALIGHIERI (C. 1265–1321)

I N *THE DIVINE COMEDY*, ITALIAN POET DANTE Alighieri explores "both the worst and best of which human beings are capable," writes scholar Robin Kirkpatrick. "Outwardly, Dante aims to investigate nothing less than the whole of the physical and spiritual universe."

Completed just before his death in 1321, the poem begins with the Roman poet Virgil guiding Dante through **hell** and purgatory. Then Beatrice, a woman whom Dante loved and respected from afar, guides him through **heaven**. Poems in the ancient world were called comedies if they tended to have happy endings and were written in everyday languages, such as Italian, rather than Latin.

As Dante descends into the underworld, he sees sinners who are punished in particular ways in accordance with their sins. For example, fortune-tellers must walk with their heads on backward, unable to see what lies ahead. The gluttonous are forced to eat excrement. The bodies of thieves are entwined with snakes or serpents. Physically, Dante's hell also features the rivers Acheron and Styx from the **Hades** of ancient Greek mythology. Hell also is depicted as a gigantic funnel that leads to the center of the earth, where Satan resides for all eternity. The sinners who were least evil reside in the upper levels or circles of hell; the most grievous sinners reside closer to the earth's center. "Because this notion of balance informs all of God's chosen punishments," write the SparkNotes editors, "God's justice emerges as rigidly objective, mechanical, and impersonal . . . and punishment becomes a matter of nearly scientific formula."

After the journey through hell and the center of the earth, Dante climbs the gigantic stepped Mountain of Purgatory in the earth's southern hemisphere. Repentant sinners reside on the various ledges. At the summit of this mountain lies the Garden of Eden. As Dante finally ascends the heavenly realms, he encounters God, at which point his desire and his will "were being turned like a wheel, all at one speed, by the love which moves the sun and the other stars."

See also Heaven (c. 2400 BCE), Hades (c. 850 BCE), Hell (c. 400 BCE), Outer Darkness (c. 80 CE)

This 1465 fresco by Italian painter Domenico di Michelino (1417–1491) shows Dante holding a copy of *The Divine Comedy*, gesturing downward to the entrance to hell. In the background are the various terraces of Mount Purgatory, with the spheres of heaven above and the city of Florence to the right.

SKY BURIAL

ODORIC OF PORDENONE (1286–1331)

"THE VULTURES GATHERED ON THE MOUNTAIN-side to watch," writes journalist Seth Faison. "On the grassy slope below, a Tibetan monk placed the naked corpse of an old woman on a sacred clearing and stepped away to sharpen his knife on the side of a rock. He marched once around an old Buddhist monument, mumbling a prayer, and then he cut her body into pieces."

Welcome to the ancient practice of Tibetan sky burial—a way of disposing of a corpse by exposing it to vultures and other birds, often on a mountain. Aside from being considered a generous way of returning a body to the local creatures, it is practical, considering that the ground of mountainous Tibet is often too hard and rocky for digging a grave and trees may be scarce for building a fire for cremation. Relatives of the deceased may remain nearby but usually do not watch the practice, also known as *jhator*, in which a monk or *rogyapa* (body breaker) cuts apart the body. Even the bones are consumed by birds after being pulverized with mallets and ground with *tsampa* (a mixture of barley flower, tea, and yak butter). Although the Chinese banned Tibetan sky burials from the late 1960s until the 1980s, the practice is permitted today.

It is difficult to determine when Tibetan sky burial became a common practice. It seems to date back at least from the time of the Italian traveler Friar Odoric, who journeyed to Tibet around 1328. Although his reports contained some distortions of local customs, he did write of priests and monks who cut bodies to pieces and then described how "eagles and vultures come down from the mountains, and every one takes his morsel and carries it away."

Similar kinds of "burials" by exposure to the air and predators have been practiced by other cultures, such as some in Neolithic Britain. Also, through the centuries, followers of Zoroastrianism, an ancient Iranian religion, exposed the dead on raised structures known as Towers of Silence.

See also Cremation (c. 20,000 BCE), Ossuaries (c. 1000 BCE), *The Tibetan Book of the Dead* (c. 780), Viking Ship Burials (834)

Zoroastrian Towers of Silence in the Iranian province of Yazd.

BLACK DEATH

JEUAN GETHIN (D. 1349), IBN KHALDUN (1332–1406), SHIBASABURO KITASATO
(1853–1931), ALEXANDRE YERSIN (1863–1943), NORMAN F. CANTOR (1929–2004)

I N THE LATE FOURTEENTH CENTURY, THE ARAB historian Ibn Khaldun wrote, "Civilization both East and West was visited by a destructive plague that devastated nations and caused populations to vanish. It swallowed up many of the good things of civilization and wiped them out." Nearly 500 years later it would become known as the Black Death.

According to the historian Norman F. Cantor, "The Black Death . . . was the greatest biomedical disaster in European and possibly world history." This devastating outbreak of the bubonic plague probably began in Asia and entered Europe in 1347. According to some estimates, roughly 75 million people worldwide perished, and between one-third and two-thirds of Europe's population was wiped out. It is likely that the same disease visited Europe numerous times, with varying mortality rates, until the twentieth century. Europeans quickly developed theories about the cause of the disease that ranged from astrological forces or God's wrath to the poisoning of wells by Jews. As a result, thousands of Jews were exterminated, many by burning, as were lepers and even individuals with severe acne or psoriasis.

In 1894, the French-Swiss physician Alexandre Yersin and the Japanese physician Shibasaburo Kitasato finally elucidated the bacterial origin of bubonic plague. Although scientists still debate whether all the plagues were in fact the same disease, the cause is usually considered to be *Yersinia pestis* or its variants, which are carried by rodents and fleas. People who are infected by the plague display "buboes," or swellings of lymph nodes, and afflicted individuals die within a few days. Journalist Edward Marriott writes, "Plague. The very word carries an unholy resonance. No other disease can claim its apocalyptic power: it can lie dormant for centuries, only to resurface with nation-killing force."

See also Four Horsemen of the Apocalypse (c. 70 CE), Plague Doctor Costume (1619), Extinction (1796), Euthanasia (1872)

1347

This depiction of plague victims being blessed by a priest is from the late fourteenth-century encyclopedia *Omne Bonum*, complied in London by English clerk James le Palmer (c. 1325–1375).

BANSHEE

WILLIAM BUTLER YEATS (1865–1939)

VARIOUS CULTURES THROUGH TIME HAVE HAD legends of phenomena, beings, or animals that were harbingers of death. Birds pecking at a window, clocks that stopped, and black cats crossing one's path were believed to be omens of misfortune and death.

In Irish folklore, banshees were female spirits who wailed when someone was about to die. Through time, legends have suggested a variety of banshee forms. Early descriptions of banshees can be found in the c. 1350 publication of the *Cathreim Thoirdhealbhaigh* (*Triumphs of Turlough*) by Irish historian Sean Mac Craith. Although his work has historical value in describing the wars between the Irish and the de Clare family of Norman lords, fantastical parts describe banshees as women, one who is beautiful and others who are ugly and surrounded by mutilated bodies. The ugly banshees foretold the death of both Irish and Norman combatants. In the book, the commanders ignored the banshees and continued fighting, leading to more death. In many legends, banshees warned only special families, such as those of pure Irish descent.

Various Celtic countries have had similar death-omen legends involving lights, candles, and flames that were said to travel, near the ground, on the route from the cemetery to the home of a dying person and then back to the cemetery. The terms *will-o'-wisp* and *corpse fire* referred to lights within graveyards that were omens of death and that also might show the route of a future funeral. Related bansheelike creatures from nearby regions include the *bean nighe*, a Scottish female fairy often considered an omen of death. According to legend, these beings wander by streams, where they wash the clothing of those who are about to die.

Of these kinds of beings, Irish poet W. B. Yeats wrote in 1893, "He had many strange sights. . . . I asked him had he ever seen the faeries. . . . I asked too if he had ever seen the banshee. 'I have seen it,' he said, 'down there by the water, batting the river with its hands.'"

See also The Witch of Endor (c. 1007 BCE), Ghosts (c. 100 CE), Séance (1848)

"Bunworth Banshee," from *Fairy Legends and Traditions of the South of Ireland* (1834) by the Irish antiquary Thomas Crofton Croker (1798–1854).

Le Petit Journal

ADMINISTRATION
61, RUE LAFAYETTE, 61

Les manuscrits ne sont pas rendus

On s'abonne sans frais
dans tous les bureaux de poste

5 CENT. SUPPLÉMENT ILLUSTRÉ **5** CENT.

23ᵐᵉ Année — ✶✶ — Numéro 1.150

DIMANCHE 1ᵉʳ DÉCEMBRE 1912

ABONNEMENTS

	SIX MOIS	UN AN
SEINE et SEINE-ET-OISE..	2 fr.	3 fr. 50
DÉPARTEMENTS.............	2 fr.	4 fr. »
ÉTRANGER	2 50	5 fr. »

LE CHOLÉRA

GRIM REAPER

ALBRECHT DÜRER (1471-1528)

"FROM THE BRONZE AGE TO THE ATOMIC AGE, death has been personified and symbolized artistically in a variety of ways," writes psychologist Lewis R. Aiken. These depictions range from large black vulturelike birds attacking headless human corpses in Neolithic settlements in today's Turkey to the Rider on a Pale Horse in the Book of Revelation of the New Testament. Perhaps the best-known depiction of death in the West is the Grim Reaper, a hooded skeletal figure carrying a large scythe—an image that appeared around the fourteenth century with the Black Plague and became common from the fifteenth century onward. The scythe, a tool with a blade for cutting crops, became the metaphor for the "harvest" of millions who died in Europe during the plagues.

Similar skeletal depictions include the 1424 *danse macabre* ("dance of death") painted on a wall of the Cemetery of the Saint Innocents in Paris. Other images of people dancing with skeletons served to remind viewers that death was always nearby. These kinds of renditions also were known as memento mori (Latin for "remember you must die"). Another famous rendition of the Grim Reaper, riding an emaciated horse, appears in a 1505 drawing by German engraver Albrecht Dürer.

Personifications of death involving skeletal components appear in many cultures. The Irish have the *dullahan*, a decapitated rider on a black horse who has a whip made from a human spine. In Poland, death sometimes has been represented by an old skeletal woman. San La Muerte (Saint Death) is a male skeletal folk saint that is venerated in South America, and the similar Santa Muerte—also known as Our Lady of the Holy Death and depicted as a female skeletal creature—is venerated in Mexico. Interestingly, in 2013, a high-ranking Vatican official proclaimed that this Mexican folk "death saint" is a blasphemous symbol that should not be part of any religion.

See also Yama (c. 1100 BCE), Four Horsemen of the Apocalypse (c. 70 CE), *Death and the Miser* (c. 1490), Day of the Dead (1519), Plague Doctor Costume (1619), Death's-Head Hawk Moth (1846), *The Garden of Death* (1896)

This illustration in *Le Petit Journal* (December 1912) shows the Grim Reaper bringing death by cholera to the masses.

DEATH AND THE MISER

HIERONYMUS BOSCH (C. 1450–1516)

☠

ACCORDING TO ART HISTORIAN WALTER BOSING, Netherlandish painter Hieronymus Bosch presents viewers with "a world of dreams [and] nightmares in which forms seem to flicker and change before our eyes." Often filled with fantastic figures that depict religious or moral themes, each of the paintings becomes a puzzle to explore. Erwin Pankofsky writes in *Early Netherlandish Painting*, "In spite of all the ingenious, erudite, and in part extremely useful research devoted to the task of 'decoding Bosch,' I cannot help feeling that the real secret of his magnificent nightmares and daydreams has still to be disclosed. We have bored a few holes through the door of the locked room; but somehow we do not seem to have discovered the key."

Death and the Miser, painted by Bosch around 1490, is a kind of memento mori ("remember you must die") work depicting the inevitably of death. The painting shows a dying man who is forced to choose between spiritual and material riches. A demon appears to be offering or taking a bag of coins, and an angel beckons upward to a crucifix and a beam of light. Death, in the form of a robed skeleton, points an arrow toward the man,

indicating that his day of judgment has come. In the foreground, we see a depiction of a miser storing gold in a chest while clutching a rosary, and some interpretations suggest that this miser is the dying man himself at a previous stage in life. Several other demonic figures and imps in the man's room may be there to taunt him and steal his treasures. Ultimately, the viewer cannot discern whether the dying man will embrace the angel's offering of light and salvation over money and earthly concerns.

Another famous painting by Bosch is *The Garden of Earthly Delights*, a triptych in which the left panel shows God presenting Eve to Adam. The central panel is a complex and puzzling scene that includes nude people, odd animals, large fruits, and other mysterious objects. The right panel is a hellish dark realm also filled with people and enigmatic creatures. This series of panels warns viewers of the fiery **hell** that awaits those who overindulge in life's pleasures.

See also Hell (c. 400 BCE), Dante's *The Divine Comedy* (1321), Grim Reaper (1424), Day of the Dead (1519), *The Garden of Death* (1896)

Death and the Miser (oil on panel) by Hieronymus Bosch.

C. 1490

DAY OF THE DEAD

HERNÁN CORTÉS DE MONROY Y PIZARRO (1485–1547), JOSÉ GUADALUPE POSADA
(1852–1913), OCTAVIO PAZ LOZANO (1914–1998)

"IT MAY SEEM STRANGE TO THOSE FROM OTHER cultures that a festival dedicated to the dead should be a joyous occasion, but Day of the Dead is exactly that," write Kitty Williams and Stevie Mack. "Combining reverence for the dead with . . . a certain mockery of death itself, Day of the Dead is a vibrant and colorful celebration of life."

Day of the Dead is a Mexican holiday in which observers remember those who have died. Taking place mostly on November 1 and November 2—and celebrated in Spain, much of Latin America, and other countries—the tradition includes building private altars honoring the dead and inviting the souls of the departed into the home, accompanied by the ubiquitous presence of sugar skulls and vibrant orange marigold flowers. Graves are visited, cleaned, and decorated with *ofrendas* (offerings).

The beginnings of this celebration may date back to Aztec festivals dedicated to the goddess Mictecacihuatl, queen of the underworld and "Lady of the Dead." The modern version of the holiday fuses these ancient nature-based pre-Hispanic traditions with the Catholic feasts of All Saints' (Hallows') Day (a celebration to honor all the saints) and All Souls' Day (commemorating all those who have died and now are in purgatory), a process that began after the Spanish conquistador Hernán Cortés entered Mexico in 1519 and continued as Catholicism gradually became the dominant religion. By the middle of the 1700s, Mexican Day of the Dead celebrations largely resembled today's practices. In the twentieth century, *La Calavera Catrina* (The Elegant Skull)—a Mictecacihuatl-inspired etching by the Mexican printmaker José Guadalupe Posada—became an icon for the festival.

According to the Mexican writer Octavio Paz, "The word death is not pronounced in New York, in Paris, in London, because it burns the lips. The Mexican, in contrast, is familiar with death, jokes about it, caresses it, sleeps with it, celebrates it; it is one of his favorite toys and his most steadfast love. . . . Death is not hidden away. . . ."

See also Xibalba (c. 100 BCE), Grim Reaper (1424), *Death and the Miser* (c. 1490), Funeral Processions (c. 1590), Ghost Dance (1890), *The Garden of Death* (1896)

Statuettes of "La Calavera Catrina," an icon of Day of the Dead celebrations that also satirizes the Mexican upper class.

GOLEM

JUDAH LOEW BEN BEZALEL (C. 1520-1609)

A GOLEM FROM JEWISH FOLKLORE IS AN animated humanlike creature, crafted from clay or mud, that crosses the eerie boundaries between life and death and between consciousness and unconsciousness while raising questions about free will and the hazards of playing God. Probably the most famous golem is the one that the sixteenth-century Prague rabbi Judah Loew ben Bezalel allegedly created to defend the Jews of the Prague ghetto from anti-Semitic attacks in 1580. The golem, known as Yossele, possessed the power to make himself invisible and to summon spirits from the dead, though he could not be animated during the Shabbat.

A golem usually is inscribed with magical or religious words that keep it animated. For example, according to legend, golem creators sometimes wrote the name of God on the golem's forehead or on a clay tablet or paper under its tongue. Other golems were animated by the word *emet* ("truth" in the Hebrew language) written on their foreheads. If the first letter in *emet* is erased to form *met* ("death" in Hebrew), the golem can be deactivated. Some other old Jewish recipes for creating a golem required a person to combine each letter of the Hebrew alphabet with each letter from the *tetragrammaton* (YHVH), the Hebrew name of God, and pronounce each of the resulting letter pairs with every possible vowel sound. The tetragrammaton serves as an "activation word" to pierce reality and energize the being.

The word *golem* appears only once in the Bible (Psalms 139:16), where it refers to an imperfect or unformed body. The New International Version translates the verse as "Your eyes saw my unformed body; all the days ordained for me were written in your book before one of them came to be." In Hebrew today, *golem* often signifies something that is "brainless" or "helpless." As such, most golems in literature were dumb but could be made to perform simple, repetitive tasks. In fact, the challenge for the golem creator was to determine how to stop the golem from carrying out or repeating a task.

See also Terra-Cotta Army (c. 210 BCE), Resurrection (c. 30 CE), *Frankenstein* (1818), Walking Corpse Syndrome (1880), Lovecraft's Reanimator (1922), Zombies (1968)

Rabbi Loew and Golem (1899) by prolific Czech artist Mikoláš Aleš (1852-1913).

FUNERAL PROCESSIONS

"IT CAN BE ARGUED THAT HUMANS STARTED becoming human the first time they added items to a grave" writes author Katy Benjamin. In the entry on **Natufian funeral flowers** (c. 11,000 BCE), we encountered graves lined with flowers, along with evidence of feasting at some burials. From early times, diverse peoples had a connection with the dead, who often were shown respect with funeral procession rites. For instance, people in funeral processions for prominent individuals in ancient Rome sometimes wore masks with images of the family's dead ancestors, and in many cultures professional female mourners were hired to wail loudly. In contrast, from the 1600s through the 1800s, Europeans sometimes hired "funeral mutes" with dark clothing and sad faces.

Interestingly, through history, "corpse roads" were the common pathways for moving corpses to their final burial places. According to folklore, fairies, wraiths, and various kinds of spirits of the dead also traveled along special routes called "church-way paths," which Shakespeare linked to the physical corpse roads of yore. In the bard's *A Midsummer Night's Dream*, written around 1590, Puck, a clever elf or sprite, says, "Now it is the time of night / That the graves, all gaping wide, / Every one lets forth his sprite, / In the church-way paths to glide."

Today, the Christian funeral procession or cortege follows a eulogy and, sometimes, a *visitation* (also called a wake, or viewing) in which the body of a deceased person is displayed in a casket. In many Western countries, the deceased are transported from the funeral home to a place of worship or cemetery in a specialized vehicle called a hearse. A New Orleans jazz funeral may employ a march with a jazz band, the music of which becomes more upbeat after the final ceremony at the **cemetery**. Hindu processions from the deceased's home to the **cremation** site are an all-male affair, with the chief mourner (usually the oldest son) lighting the funeral pyre.

"Funeral rites can be studied to increase understanding of cultural values related to death," writes educator Bill Hoy, "to discover a perspective on how people make meaning of loss, and to increase awareness of how people from that cultural group support one another through ritual in the aftermath of a loved person's death."

See also Cremation (c. 20,000 BCE), Natufian Funeral Flowers (c. 11,000 BCE), Coffins (c. 4000 BCE), Viking Ship Burials (834), Banshee (c. 1350) Day of the Dead (1519), Cemeteries (1831), Embalming (1867)

The Funeral Procession of Love (c. 1580) by French painter Henri Lerambert (c. 1550–1609).

Der. Doctor Schna- bel von Rom

Vos Creditis, als eine fabel,
quod scribitur vom Doctor schnabel,
der fugit die Contagion
et autert seinen Lohn darvon.
Cadavera sucht er zu fristen,
gleich wie der Corvus auf der Misten.
Ah Credite, ziehet nicht dort hin,
dann Romæ regnat die Pestin.

Quis non deberet sehr erschrec
für seiner Virgul oder stecken,
qua loquitur, als wär er stumm
und deutet sein Consilium.
Wie mancher Credit ohne zweyfel
das ihn tentir ein schwarzen Teuffel.
Marsupium heist seine Höll,
und aurum die geholte seel.

I. Columbina, ad vivum delineavit.   Paulus Fürst. Excud.

Kleidung wider den Tod zü Rom. Anno 1656.
Also gehen die Doctores Medici daher zü Rom, wann sie die an der Pest erkranckte Personen besuchen, sie zü curiren und fragen, sich vor dem Gifft zü sichern, ein langes Kleid von gewäxtem Tuch ihr Angesicht ist verlarvt, für den Augen haben sie grosse Crystalline Brillen, vor der Nasen einen langen Schnabel voll wolriechender Specerey, in der Hände, welche mit Handschuhen wol versehen ist, eine lange Ruthe und darmit deuten sie, was man thün, und gebrauchen soll.

PLAGUE DOCTOR COSTUME

CHARLES DE LORME (1584–1678)

"BEING BORN IN MEDIEVAL EUROPE WAS LIKE losing the historical lottery," writes health-policy expert Jackie Rosenhek. "Superstition reigned [and] misery was the rule . . . among the long-suffering serfs." The people knew "disease and hunger intimately," feared "the wrath of a vengeful God," and often died young.

Plague doctors were special medical "physicians" who attempted to treat the poor during the time of the **Black Death**, which killed more than 75 million people and peaked in Europe around 1350. Although many of the plague doctors had little training, they were paid by various cities to tend to those in need, to keep records of the deaths, and sometimes to help oversee wills. In the seventeenth and eighteenth centuries, some plague doctors wore beaklike masks filled with aromatic substances such as lavender, roses, carnations, mint, spices, camphor, ambergris, cloves, myrrh, and vinegar. This was an age before the scientific discovery of disease-causing germs, and bad smells often were associated with "miasmas," which were thought to cause disease that might be warded off by the aromas in the beak masks. Alas, plague doctors could do little to help the afflicted. Many of them practiced bloodletting or placed frogs on buboes: the lymph node swellings on bubonic plague victims.

The scary beak costumes were adopted by the French physician Charles de Lorme in 1619, and they often consisted of a long waxed protective overcoat, a mask with glass eyeholes, and a wide-brimmed leather hat or hood. The beak could hold straw to filter the putrid "bad air." The plague doctors carried wooden canes to help examine patients without direct contact.

Although de Lorme lived to age 96, a notable accomplishment in a time of epidemics, his famous costume probably did not significantly prevent the spread of the disease. Rosenhek writes, "The beak doctors, as they came to be known, dropped like flies or pretty much lived under constant quarantine, wandering the countryside and city streets like pariahs . . . until of course desperate families needed them."

See also Four Horsemen of the Apocalypse (c. 70 CE), Black Death (1347), Grim Reaper (1424), Gravediggers (1651), Extinction (1796), Euthanasia (1872)

This c. 1656 copper engraving—published and possibly created by the German book and art dealer Paul Fürst (1608–1666)—depicts Doctor Schnabel ("Doctor Beak"), a Roman plague doctor wearing protective attire that was typical around this time.

CHILDREN
AND CAPACOCHA

"IMAGINE YOU ARE AN INCA CHILD BEING PREPARED for sacrifice, or *capacocha* (kah-pah-KOH-cha), selected because you are attractive and have no blemishes. As the time for your death grows near on a high Andean mountain, you may be drugged with coca leaves and given a corn-based beer called *chicha*. Finally, you are placed in a shaftlike tomb and walled in alive, left to die in the freezing temperatures. Or perhaps you were killed by strangulation or a blow to the head.

Welcome to the strange and chilling realm of the Inca, the powerful civilization that arose in Peru sometime in the thirteenth century. Such sacrifices were performed around important events, such as after an earthquake or the death of an emperor or during a famine. This entry is dated to 1622, the year in which Spanish writer and priest Rodrigo Hernández Principe provided an account of Tanta Carhua, a 10-year-old girl who was taken to the emperor in the Inca capital, Cusco, before being led to the mountains, where she was sacrificed. In the 1990s, several mummies of sacrificed Inca children with ages ranging from about 6 to 15 were found on Mount Llullaillaco, Argentina, in a state of good preservation as a result of the cold.

Other Native American cultures also practiced child sacrifice. For example, Maya art depicts the removal of children's hearts when a king ascended the throne or on other special occasions. Decapitated children have been found in the ruins of the Toltecs. The Aztecs sacrificed young children who were in great pain so that their tears would wet the earth, and they sometimes ate them. The Pawnee people of North America practiced the Morning Star ceremony each spring, in which a captured young girl was held for a few months and then sacrificed. The Pawnee believed that the blood from her various arrow wounds would soak the ground to produce a fertile soil. On April 22, 1838, Haxti, a 14-year-old Oglala Lakota girl, was the last Pawnee sacrifice.

See also Terra-Cotta Army (c. 210 BCE), Xibalba (c. 100 BCE), Ghost Dance (1890), Kamikaze Pilots (1944)

The well-preserved "Plomo Mummy" was discovered on the Cerro El Plomo mountain peak in the Andes in 1954. Subsequent analysis showed that this young boy, who was sacrificed by the Inca 500 years ago, was from a wealthy family. This replica, showing typical idols and keepsakes that accompanied child sacrifices, is on display at the National Museum of Natural History in Santiago, Chile.

GRAVEDIGGERS

MIQUEL PARETS (1610–1661)

IQUEL PARETS, A TANNER ACTIVE IN LOCAL Barcelona politics, kept a diary that included his vivid descriptions of gravediggers during a horrible bubonic plague outbreak in 1651. In particular, Parets describes carts traveling through the city, collecting corpses that were often "thrown from the windows into the street" and then carted away by the gravediggers, "who go about playing their guitars [and] tambourines . . . in order to forget such grave afflictions, the memory alone of which is enough to want to be done with this wretched life. . . ." After the carts were filled, the gravediggers buried the corpses in a field called the beanfield near a monastery. When the carts were filled, stretchers were used, and the gravediggers often would "carry dead babies or other children gravely ill with the plague on their backs." Paret himself lost his wife and three of his children to the plague.

In the past, many cultures considered gravediggers "unclean." In Japan and India, for example, gravediggers often were shunned or ignored by society. In some of the Melanesian and Polynesian countries, a person who touched a corpse was not allowed to touch food for a period of time. According to author Christine Quigley, Christians overcame some of these taboos. "By considering [the body] a relic and by developing formal rituals for parting with it and disposing of it, they allowed the clergy and laity to touch and even kiss the dead without fear."

In the eighteenth and nineteenth centuries, gravediggers' intimate knowledge of the location and freshness of buried corpses coaxed some of them to accept bribes from body snatchers who sought corpses for anatomical research. In modern times, gravediggers can be volunteers, relatives of the deceased, temporary laborers, professionals, or—in the case of churchyards—sextons. Some graves are dug by hand with shovels, and in industrialized countries a backhoe often is used.

See also Gravestones (c. 1600 BCE), Plague Doctor Costume (1619), Sin-Eaters (1825), Cemeteries (1831), Resurrectionists (1832), Schwabe's *The Death of the Gravedigger* (1895)

A gravedigger holds the skull of "poor Yorick" in a famous scene from the play *Hamlet* by William Shakespeare (1564–1616). This 1839 painting, *Hamlet and Horatio in the Cemetery*, is by French artist Eugène Delacroix (1798–1863).

THE LATE MR. R. W. THOMSON, C.E., OF EDINBURGH.

family seat in Nottinghamshire. He re-
fused the usual retiring pension. Lor
Ossington had married, in July, 182
Lady Charlotte Cavendish Bentinck, thir
daughter of William, fourth Duke of Por
land ; but by his marriage had no issu
His title, therefore, has become extinc
Several of his Lordship's brothers rose
eminence in their respective profession

The Portrait of Lord Ossington is from
photograph by Mr. Mayall, of Regen
street.

THE LATE MR. R. W. THOMSON

This distinguished Scottish engineer w
inventor of the locomotive traction stea
engine, with broad indiarubber tires on th
driving wheels, for use on common road
also of the portable steam-crane and th
elliptic rotary engine, as well as of an in
proved hydraulic floating dock ; and son
of his inventions have, from time to tim
been described in our Journal. He died
Edinburgh on the 8th inst., in the fifty-fir
year of his age, having been born in 182
at Stonehaven, where his father had estab
lished a factory. In early youth he showe
great talents for mechanical science, an
after spending two years of his boyhood i
America, served a practical apprenticeshi
in workshops at Aberdeen and Dundee, fo
lowed by learning the profession of a civ
engineer at Glasgow, and subsequently wit
his cousin, Mr. Lyon, builder of the Dea
Bridge at Edinburgh. He was employe
in the blasting of Dunbar Castle, and i
that of Dover Cliff, where he first applie
the method of firing mines by electricity
He next passed into the employment of th
Stephensons, as a railway engineer in th
Eastern Counties. In 1852 he went t
Java, to erect the machinery of a sugar
plantation, which he greatly improved, and
becoming a partner in the estate, reside
there till 1862, when he came home an
settled at Edinburgh. The portrait i
from a photograph by Mr. Peterson, o
Copenhagen.

OBITUARIES

JOHN NICHOLS (1745–1826)

AFTER YOU DIE, WILL THE WORLD REMEMBER anything you did? Most of us will never have our lives illuminated in a *New York Times* obituary or discussed by a TV news anchorperson. Your great-grandchildren may carry some vestigial memory of you, but that will fade like a burning ember when they die—and you may well be extinguished and forgotten.

Obituaries (from the Latin *obitus*, meaning "departure" or "death") are usually news articles that provide details of the life of a person who has died recently. Of course, death notifications and information preceded the rise of newspapers. For example, in many European nations, death sometimes was announced by the tolling of bells, and funeral notices were posted on the windows of buildings. Additionally, many medieval community churches maintained necrologies, which sometimes included information on the title, parentage, or origin of the deceased and were consulted during the commemoration prayers at chapter meetings.

Among the first modern obituaries in periodicals were those which appeared in the London-based *The Gentleman's Magazine* (founded 1731), which established a standard for many periodicals to come—particularly when under the editorship of John Nichols, beginning in 1778. Researchers can learn a lot from obituaries because they tend to reflect what cultures value and want to remember about the deceased as well as offering glimpses of the relative societal roles of men and women. According to the educator Janice Hume, obituaries "contribute to a society's well-being by strengthening it collectively and by highlighting the importance of its individual members."

Today, obituaries still have a popular following. David Bowman, a former editor in chief of the *Sydney Morning Herald*, notes, "Perhaps in an age of bewildering change, it buoys one up to discover how others survived their times. The best obituaries, after all, capture life; they are not about death."

See also Epitaphs (c. 480 BCE), Death Certificate (1770), Last Words of the Dying (1922)

An obituary for Scottish inventor Robert Thomson (1822–1873) that appeared in *The Illustrated London News*, one of the world's first illustrated weekly news magazines, on March 29, 1873. Thomson was famous for inventions dealing with tires and steam engines.

Behayn. inu.   Andr. Stoc. Sculp.

AUTOPSY

FREDERICK II OF HOHENSTAUFEN (1194–1250), GIOVANNI BATTISTA MORGAGNI (1682–1771), CARL VON ROKITANSKY (1804–1878), RUDOLF LUDWIG KARL VIRCHOW (1821–1902)

"AFTER MY DEATH, I WISH YOU TO DO AN autopsy," Napoleon Bonaparte said to his physician. "Make a detailed report to my son. Indicate to him what remedies or mode of life he can pursue that will prevent his suffering. . . . This is very important, for my father died . . . with symptoms very much like mine." Napoleon had been experiencing vomiting and fever, and his autopsy revealed stomach cancer.

An autopsy is a medical procedure involving a careful examination of a corpse, often to determine the cause of death. One of the earliest and most famous laws authorizing human dissection in Europe was introduced by the Holy Roman Emperor Frederick II in 1240. Italian anatomist Giovanni Morgagni became well known for autopsies that correlated symptoms with organic changes, and he published hundreds of reports in his 1761 *De sedibus et causis morborum* (*On the Seats and Causes of Disease*), which included descriptions of coronary artery disease, pneumonia, and various cancers. The Bohemian physician Carl von Rokitansky performed many thousands of autopsies using a definite protocol, making autopsy a separate branch of medicine. German pathologist Rudolf Virchow emphasized the importance of the microscope to study autopsy tissues.

Today, a physician makes a large incision along the front of the body, and many of the organs may initially be removed together as one large mass. Major blood vessels are opened and inspected. Stomach and intestinal contents sometimes give an indication of the time of death. A Stryker electric saw is used to open the skull and expose the brain. Specialized techniques may be used that include electron microscopy, radiology, and toxicology (to check for poisons).

Although autopsies have often revealed diagnostic errors and unexpected findings about the cause of death, since around 1960 the number of autopsies performed in Western countries has been declining greatly, perhaps partly because of physicians' fear of malpractice lawsuits. The incidence of autopsies varies with nationality and religion; Judaism and Islam generally do not encourage widespread use of autopsies.

See also Cremation (c. 20,000 BCE), Mummies (c. 5050 BCE), Death Certificate (1770), Resurrectionists (1832), Embalming (1867), Cryonics (1962)

The Anatomical Lecture by Dutch painter and engraver Jacob de Gheyn II (c. 1565–1629).

CITY OF NEW YORK.

STATE OF NEW YORK.
CERTIFICATE AND RECORD OF DEATH

Henry H Bliss

No. of Certificate

26382
26382

(stamp: BUREAU OF RECORDS 8 A.M. SEP 16)

This is to certify that I, JACOB E. BAUGH, Coroner in and for the Borough of MANHATTAN have, this _14_ day of _Sept_ 189_9_, taken charge of the body of _deceased_ found at _Riverside_ _thof_ in the _____ Ward of said Borough, and that an inquest thereon is pending

Jacob E Baugh Coroner

I hereby certify that I have viewed the body of the deceased, and from _examination_ and evidence, that he died on the _14_ day of _Sept_ 189_9_, a _6.20_ A.M., and that the cause of his death was

Fracture of Skull
Hæmorrhage Cerebral
Overrun by an automobile

Place of Burial, _Cedar Grove_
Date of Burial, _Sept 16 1899_
Undertaker, _Keating & Hermann_
Residence, _235 & Ave._

Philip F. O'Hanlon M. D.
_121 W 96 St_
Coroner's Physician.

Date of Record.	Indirect Cause of Death.	Direct Cause of Death.	Class of Dwell'g (A "tenement" being a house occupied by more than two families.)	Last place of Residence.	Place of Death.	Mother's Birthplace.	Mother's Name.	Father's Birthplace.	Father's Name.	How long Resident in New York City.	How long in U. S., if foreign born.	Place of Birth.	Occupation.	Single, Married or Widowed.	Color.	Age.	Name.	Date of Death.
	H Bliss	Private	235 W 75 St	Central Park West						Life		United States	Merchant	Married	White	624	Henry H Bliss	9/14/99

DEATH CERTIFICATE

"IT IS ONE OF A DOCTOR'S MOST IMPORTANT FINAL acts in caring for a patient, even though the patient is no longer around to appreciate it," writes Lawrence Altman, MD, referring to the death certificate, a document that has many benefits for society, including "establishing a legal basis for life insurance and estate settlements; providing critical information to survivors and descendants in an era of burgeoning advances in genetics; advancing knowledge about diseases, accidents and other causes of death. . . ."

In the United States, the death certificate usually starts its own life when a medical practitioner certifies that a person has died. The certificate is sent to the responsible local government office, which transmits the information to a register of vital statistics. It may be required before burial or cremation and may contain information such as the date, the location, the immediate cause of death, and other conditions that contributed to the death. Because trained individuals generally are required to complete the death certificate, this may help prevent murder cover-ups.

Before the 1800s, churches often maintained records of burials in the United States and Europe, but eventually local governments began to issue death certificates. The earliest U.S. state to initiate death certificate registration was Vermont in 1770, followed by New Hampshire in 1840.

Public health officials can use death certificates to look for patterns of disease, such as the occurrence of cancers. Unfortunately, U.S. studies have shown that causes of death are often misreported on certificates, partly as a result of lack of training of resident doctors or pressure to enter a cause of death even if the residents did not know the patients very well. Entering a cause such as "cardiac arrest" provides no useful information because all hearts stop at death. Careful attention to the cause of death is important for detecting trends in disease and violence. The surgeon Barbara A. Wexelman underscores the importance of death certificates to society: "We owe it to our patients to be able to accurately record why they die . . . to help the living."

See also Epitaphs (c. 480 BCE), Obituaries (1731), Autopsy (1761)

Death certificate of Henry H. Bliss (1830–1899), the first person killed in a motor vehicle accident in the United States. As he was leaving a streetcar in New York City, he was struck by an electric-powered taxicab.

GUILLOTINE

ANTOINE LOUIS (1723–1792), JOSEPH-IGNACE GUILLOTIN (1738–1814), NICOLAS JACQUES
PELLETIER (D. 1792), HAMIDA DJANDOUBI (C. 1949–1977)

"MY MACHINE WILL TAKE OFF A HEAD IN A twinkling, and the victim will feel nothing but a refreshing coolness," physician Joseph-Ignace Guillotin stated to the French Assembly in 1789. "We cannot make too much haste, gentlemen, to allow the nation to enjoy this advantage." Although Dr. Guillotin was not the inventor of this famous decapitation device with its falling blade, he did promote its use as a humane method of execution in France—a method that actually was used in that country until 1977, when Tunisian immigrant and convicted murderer Hamida Djandoubi became the last person to be executed by this apparatus.

Other similar kinds of beheading devices predated the guillotine, such as the English "Halifax Gibbet," the Scottish "Maiden," and the Italian "Mannaia." A criminal court officer named Laquiante, engineer Tobias Schmidt, and surgeon Antoine Louis are credited with designing the prototype guillotine in France, and the first execution by guillotine was performed on the criminal Nicolas Jacques Pelletier in 1792. At least 16,000 executions followed, often with little or no justification, during France's Reign of Terror. Those executed included the nobility, intellectuals, politicians, and commoners. In Nazi Germany and Austria, another 16,000 people were guillotined between 1933 and 1945.

Imagine the horror as people were forced to put their necks into the bloody yokes of the guillotine and heard the rumbling of the heavy descending blade. Before the use of the guillotine in France, more dreadful methods were employed, such as decapitation by sword or ax (which sometime required multiple blows), hanging (which could take minutes), and quartering (in which a prisoner was hacked apart by blades or torn apart by horses tied to the person's limbs). Often, the most painful forms of execution were used on the poor.

In France, executions were a popular form of entertainment for cheering parents, who brought their children to watch. "A guillotine craze swept through France," writes author Geoffrey Abbott. "Toy manufacturers made small models of it as playthings for children. . . . The young ladies of Paris wore guillotine-shaped silver ear-rings and brooches."

See also Capital Punishment (c. 1772 BCE), Electric Chair (1890), Genocide (1944)

The 1794 execution of French political leader Maximilien Robespierre and his supporters by guillotine marked the end of the Reign of Terror that followed the French Revolution.

EXTINCTION

JEAN LÉOPOLD NICOLAS FRÉDÉRIC (GEORGES) CUVIER (1769–1832)

SPECIES USUALLY FADE FROM THE WORLD "quietly," and so we cannot be sure of their "expiration date" except for rare examples such as the thylacine, or Tasmanian tiger. That creature became extinct on September 7, 1936, in the Tasmanian Hobart Zoo when the last known specimen died of neglect. More than 99 percent of all species that ever lived are in fact extinct. The biologist Edward O. Wilson has controversially speculated that half of all plant and animal species alive today could be extinct by the end of the century because of habitat destruction, pollution, climate change, and other factors.

In a 1796 paper discussing observations based on fossil studies, the French naturalist Georges Cuvier promoted the concept of animal extinctions resulting from periodic catastrophic floods, which was a radical and threatening idea at the time. Through the millennia, species have come and gone, in part because of changing ecological conditions, global calamitous events, competition from other organisms, and related factors. A typical species usually becomes extinct within about 10 million years of its initial appearance, although this duration can vary substantially depending on the creature under consideration. The coelacanth fish was considered to have been extinct for millions of years until it was found in 1938 off the African coast, for example.

Scientists are aware of at least five mass extinctions in the history of life on earth. These extinctions involve a widespread and rapid decrease of life, often identified by a rapid change in the diversity of macroscopic (e.g., easily observable) creatures. For example, 66 million years ago, during the Cretaceous–Tertiary (K–T) extinction, roughly three-quarters of plant and animal species on earth disappeared, including the nonavian dinosaurs. The extinction probably was caused in part by the impact of a large comet or asteroid and the resultant diminution in light. Of course, mass extinctions cannot always be considered undesirable for the world, as humans and many other mammals would not have evolved without the K–T extinction.

See also Black Death (1347), Ghost Dance (1890), Genocide (1944), Death of Universe (>100 Trillion)

Painting of a dodo—an extinct flightless bird from the island of Mauritius in the Indian Ocean—by Flanders-born artist Roelant Savery (1576-1639). Ornithologist George Edwards later gave the painting to the British Museum.

JACOB'S DREAM

PHILO OF ALEXANDRIA (C. 20 BCE–C. 50 CE), WILLIAM BLAKE (1757–1827)

"BELOVED BY CHILDREN AND PAINTERS, extravagantly allegorized through the history of biblical interpretation and an inspiration to hymn writers, the evocative image of Jacob's ladder is mentioned only once in the Bible." The authors of the *Dictionary of Biblical Imagery* note that the upward and downward movement of **angels** suggests "the two ways in which humans interact with God— by receiving what God sends to earth and by aspiring upward toward God in **heaven**." The famous image of Jacob's ladder occurs in Genesis 28 when Jacob has a dream after coming to Haran:

> He dreamed, and behold, there was a ladder set up on the earth, and the top of it reached to heaven; and behold, the angels of God were ascending and descending on it! And behold, the Lord stood above it and said, "I am the Lord, the God of Abraham. . . . The land on which you lie I will give to you and to your descendants. . . ." Then Jacob awoke . . . and said, "Surely the Lord is in this place. . . ." And he was afraid and said, "This is none other than the house of God, and this is the gate of heaven."

Countless explanations of Jacob's ladder have been advanced over the centuries, with the ladder representing the interplay between the heavenly and human realms. The Jewish philosopher Philo of Alexandria provided several interpretations, one of which suggested that the angels on the ladder may represent souls descending to and ascending from bodies in a process almost reminiscent of **reincarnation**. In the New Testament, Jesus alludes to Jacob's dream when he tells followers that they "will see heaven opened, and the angels of God ascending and descending upon the Son of man" (John 1:51).

This entry is dated to c. 1805, the date of one of the most famous and inspirational renditions of Jacob's ladder by English poet and painter William Blake. Here Jacob is depicted at the foot of a spiral staircase with angelic beings.

See also Reincarnation (c. 600 BCE), Angels (c. 380), Bifrost (c. 1220), *The Wounded Angel* (1903)

Jacob's Dream (c. 1805) by English painter William Blake.

FRANKENSTEIN.

*"By the glimmer of the half-extinguished
light, I saw the dull, yellow eye of the
creature open; it breathed hard, and a
convulsive motion agitated its limbs,
*** I rushed out of the room.".*

T. Holst, del.

W. Chevalier, sculp.

FRANKENSTEIN

GIOVANNI ALDINI (1762–1834), MARY SHELLEY
(NÉE MARY WOLLSTONECRAFT GODWIN, 1797–1851)

THE AUTHOR MARY SHELLEY "WOULD BE surrounded by death, intrigue, and storm from the start," writes biology professor Michael Goldman, referring in part to the awesome lightning storm in London on the night of her birth. "While natural philosophers were learning to master electricity, others saw their efforts as sacrilegious and the angry thunderstorms a sign of God's wrath." A few days after giving birth, Mary's mother died from infection.

Death is a prominent theme in Mary Shelly's 1818 novel *Frankenstein; or, The Modern Prometheus*, which is about a scientist named Victor Frankenstein who robs slaughterhouses and cemeteries to construct a creature from various parts, which he then animates with "a spark of life." He reflects: "Life and death appeared to me ideal bounds, which I should first break through, and pour a torrent of light into our dark world. A new species would bless me as its creator. . . . I thought, that if I could bestow animation upon lifeless matter, I might . . . renew life where death had apparently devoted the body to corruption." The basic story idea came to Mary

Shelley in a dream, and she finished the novel at age nineteen. Europeans were fascinated by theories about the role of electricity in biology and the potential for reanimation of dead tissue. For example, Italian physicist Giovanni Aldini participated in many public attempts at human reanimation through electricity around 1803 in London.

Death and destruction lurk everywhere in the novel as numerous characters meet their end. Notably, Victor destroys the unfinished female companion for his monster, and the monster (who is never actually referred to by the name "Frankenstein") kills Elizabeth, the scientist's new bride. Fear of death is one of the driving forces for Victor, but by the end of the novel he feels death's inevitability, having pursued his creation to the North Pole. After Victor's death, the miserable, grief-stricken creature vows to die on his own funeral pyre to erase any sign of his existence.

See also Golem (1580), Euthanasia (1872), Electric Chair (1890), Lovecraft's Reanimator (1922), Transhumanism (1957)

Frontispiece from the 1831 edition of *Frankenstein*, published in London by Colburn and Bentley.

VAMPIRES

VLAD III, PRINCE OF WALLACHIA (1431–1476), JOHN WILLIAM POLIDORI (1795–1821),
ABRAHAM "BRAM" STOKER (1847–1912)

1819

"THEY ARE OUT THERE IN THE DARK, ALWAYS watching, always hungry," muses author Jonathan Maberry. "Clerics in the churches and temples of a thousand religions have warned of unnatural monsters that wanted to corrupt or destroy mankind." The ancient Greeks had their Lamia, who devoured young children at night. The Babylonians told tales of Lilitu, a female demon who also subsisted on the blood of babies.

Although *revenants* (ghosts or animated corpses returning from the grave) have taken many forms through the ages, today the term *vampire* usually refers to folkloric creatures who feed upon the blood of the living. Some of the modern, charismatic features of vampires can be traced to the popular 1819 novella *The Vampyre* by English writer and physician John Polidori. In 1897, the Irish theater manager and novelist Bram Stoker wrote the famous Gothic horror novel *Dracula*. Some aspects of Stoker's main character were inspired by a cruel fifteenth-century Romanian prince known as Vlad the Impaler. In the 1700s and 1800s, belief in vampires was widespread in New England, and some families actually disinterred family members and removed their hearts in an attempt to prevent them from spreading disease and death among the living.

Perhaps the modern belief in vampires was stirred when people viewed corpses that appeared bloated and emitted groans or blood from the nose and mouth (resulting from the accumulation and release of gases during decomposition) or when people encountered individuals or animals with rabies, which can cause hypersensitivity to light, hypersexuality, and an urge to bite others. According to historian Eric Johnson, "What the Slavic and European vampire mythologies both have in common . . . is that they tell an important story about how people understood natural events such as death, decomposition, and the transmission of disease prior to the advent of scientific medicine. They also serve as an illustration of the anxiety present in many Christian societies over the delicate line that seemed to separate human from animal."

See also Coffins (c. 4000 BCE), *Frankenstein* (1818), Death's-Head Hawk Moth (1846), Zombies (1968)

Vampire **(1895)** by Norwegian painter Edvard Munch (1863–1944).

SIN-EATERS

THROUGHOUT HISTORY, MANY CULTURES HAVE believed that the dead can be trapped and compelled to haunt a location or to exist in a restless, unhappy, or sinful state of being. In parts of England, Scotland, and Wales, the strange ritual of sin-eating evolved to combat this limbo and may have survived until the late 1800s. A sin-eater was usually a poor person who was paid a small fee to be present at the side of a corpse, eating bread and drinking ale that either was placed on the chest of the dead person or was passed over his or her body. After saying a prayer, the sin-eater would leave, taking the sin of the deceased person with him.

The food represented the dead person's sins, and once the person was cleansed, he or she could rest in peace and enter **heaven**. By consuming the sins of the dead, the sin-eater was risking his own afterlife and sometimes was shunned. With each and every act of sin consumption, the sin-eater became increasingly "polluted" and more detestable.

Although it is difficult to determine the degree to which sin-eating took place or was embellished through various legends, many tales exist, such as the one told by Bertram S. Puckle in *Funeral Customs* (1926): "Professor Evans of the Presbyterian College, Carmarthen [Wales], actually saw a sin-eater about the year 1825. . . . Abhorred by the superstitious villagers as a thing unclean, the sin-eater cut himself off from all social intercourse with his fellow creatures by reason of the life he had chosen; he lived as a rule in a remote place by himself, and those who chanced to meet him avoided him as they would a leper. . . . Only when a death took place did they seek him out, and when his purpose was accomplished they burned the wooden bowl and platter from which he had eaten the food handed across, or placed on the corpse for his consumption."

See also Necromancy (c. 850 BCE), Hell (c. 400 BCE), Ghosts (c. 100 CE), Gravediggers (1651), Death's-Head Hawk Moth (1846)

A statue of Tlazolteotl, a sin-eating Aztec goddess. According to legend, she could cleanse souls by "eating their filth" and also could forgive sexual misdeeds.

CEMETERIES

"**B**EFORE 1831, AMERICA HAD NO CEMETERIES," writes journalist Rebecca Greenfield. "It's not that Americans didn't bury their dead—just that large, modern graveyards did not exist. But with the construction of Mount Auburn Cemetery, a large burial ground in Cambridge, Massachusetts, the movement to build cemeteries in America began."

Of course, the notion of burying the dead or preparing them in various ways dates back as least as far as Paleolithic times, between 35,000 and 135,000 years ago, when some Neanderthals carefully arranged their dead below the ground. In Neolithic times, around 13,000 years ago, the Natufians of the eastern Mediterranean created rock shelters for graves, and the Neolithic people of Jericho buried their dead beneath their house floors. Ancient Egyptians built necropolises—cities of the dead—outside their cities. Early Native Americans sometimes placed their dead in dirt burial mounds, and early Christians in Rome created underground chambers, or catacombs, for the dead. Today, Wadi Al-Salaam, an Islamic cemetery in Iraq, is thought to be the largest cemetery in the world, containing many millions of bodies.

In modern times, the term *cemetery*, from the ancient Greek word meaning "sleeping place," is typically used for parklike land specifically designated for burial, as distinct from *graveyard*, which implies an association with the property of a particular house of worship, such as a church. In the eighteenth and nineteenth centuries, crowded graveyards tended to fall out of favor in many locales because of concerns about infectious diseases and lack of space. After the 1830s in the United States people began to visit parklike cemeteries for picnics, and today cemeteries sometimes feature columbarium walls containing niches for urns that hold cremated remains.

Cemeteries fascinate Stanford professor Keith Eggener because of their liminality: The "intensification of knowledge and emotion [and] the coming together of these disparate states of life and death, nature and culture, [where] burial isn't just about celebrating the dead [but] keeping them out of the realm of the living … is why cemeteries were removed from cities."

See also Cremation (c. 20,000 BCE), Natufian Funeral Flowers (c. 11,000 BCE), Burial Mounds (c. 4000 BCE), Gravestones (c. 1600 BCE), Viking Ship Burials (834), Gravediggers (1651), Thanatourism (1996)

This angelic statue in the Monumental Cemetery of Staglieno in Genoa, Italy, reminds visitors to maintain a respectful silence. The cemetery—one of the largest in Europe—was approved for construction in 1835 and officially opened in 1851.

RESURRECTIONISTS

WILLIAM HARVEY (1578–1657), WILLIAM BURKE (1792–1829)

DURING THE EUROPEAN RENAISSANCE, SCHOLARS came to believe that dissection of human bodies was essential for furthering medical knowledge and that simply relying on ancient medical texts was insufficient. In the sixteenth and seventeenth centuries, Italy led the world in anatomical learning. However, by the 1800s, London and Edinburgh were among the hot spots for anatomical and medical breakthroughs.

To become seasoned dissectors and anatomists, surgeons of that time had to be able to suppress normal emotional responses to their human brethren. For example, the English physician William Harvey, famous for his elucidation of blood circulation, participated in dissections of both his sister and his father. In the early 1800s, the appetite for corpses was so great in England that anatomists frequently collaborated with grave robbers to secure needed specimens, as only the corpses of executed murderers could be used legally for dissection. As a result, coffin collars, mortsafes, and mort houses were employed in Scotland to prevent grave robbing.

The Anatomy Act of 1832, a United Kingdom act of Parliament, gave physicians legal access to corpses that relatives did not claim, and it became easy to obtain the corpses of poor people who died in workhouses: places where people unable to support themselves often stayed until death. This act was motivated by the growing anger at the "resurrectionists" who robbed graves for medical study, and the passage of the act was accelerated by the 1828 murders in Edinburgh by William Burke and William Hare, who strangled at least sixteen victims before selling their corpses to anatomists.

Many citizens nevertheless were angered by the act, feeling that it was unfair to the poor, whose corpses were used without their consent. Before 1832, dissection was considered a punishment for murderers, and the act therefore seemed to punish poverty. Some religious individuals felt the body should not be desecrated and buried their loved ones in lead coffins to protect them until resurrection on Judgment Day. After the act passed, riots broke out and some medical school buildings were damaged, but the lucrative trade of the resurrectionists effectively ended.

See also Resurrection (c. 30 CE), Gravediggers (1651), Autopsy (1761), "The Monkey's Paw" (1902), Lovecraft's Reanimator (1922)

This illustration of resurrectionists at work by English artist Hablot Knight Browne (1815–1882) appeared in *The Chronicles of Crime* (1887).

PREMATURE BURIAL

EDGAR ALLAN POE (1809-1849), WILLIAM TEBB (1830-1917)

EDGAR ALLAN POE, AMERICAN AUTHOR OF THE macabre, wrote in "The Premature Burial" (1844) that "no event is so terribly well adapted to inspire the supremeness of bodily and of mental distress, as is burial before death. The unendurable oppression of the lungs [and] the silence like a sea . . . —these things, with the thoughts of the air and grass above, with memory of dear friends . . . carry into the heart, which still palpitates, a degree of appalling and intolerable horror from which the most daring imagination must recoil."

Poe was both inspired and frightened by the risks of premature burial that flared in the mid-nineteenth century, when many newspaper stories reported corpses that appeared to have exhibited signs of escape attempts (such as damaged fingernails and scratch marks within the coffin) when **coffins** and tombs were reopened. For example, "The Fall of the House of Usher" (1839) describes the mental breakdown of a man who (knowingly) prematurely entombs his sister. In the end, she escapes from her tomb and bursts into his bedroom during a supernatural storm, at which point they both become corpses. In "The Cask of Amontillado" (1846), the narrator immures his colleague into a niche, using building stones and mortar, after leading him into catacombs and chaining him to a wall.

Some of these cases were apocryphal, but "apparent deaths" were not uncommon during disease epidemics and the accompanying quick burials. In 1896, businessman William Tebb cofounded the London Association for the Prevention of Premature Burial, which campaigned for burial reforms such as waiting for a body to putrefy before it was buried. Also in the 1800s, "safety coffins"—patented to decrease concerns about accidental premature burial—featured pipes that could provide air, and ringing bells to alert passersby above the ground to movement below.

The phrase *premature burial* also can refer to intentional burials used as a form of torture and execution. For example, in ancient Rome, if a Vestal Virgin violated her oath of celibacy, she was buried alive in an underground chamber with a few days of food and water. The Chinese also punished and tortured by burying people alive, as exemplified by the hundreds of thousands buried at the end of the Battle of Changping (260 BCE) and the Battle of Julu (207 BCE). More recently, Japanese soldiers buried Chinese civilians alive during the gruesome Nanking (now spelled "Nanjing") Massacre of 1937–1938.

See also Coffins (c. 4000 BCE), Gravediggers (1651), "The Raven" (1845), Cardiopulmonary Resuscitation (1956), Ondine's Curse (1962)

The Premature Burial (1854) by Belgian painter Antoine Wiertz (1806-1865).

MR HENRY LUDLOWE
IN
THE RAVEN
THE LOVE STORY OF EDGAR ALLAN POE
DIRECTION
HAZELTON & NORTH
BY GEORGE HAZELTON

"THE RAVEN"

EDGAR ALLAN POE (1809-1849)

"THE BOUNDARIES WHICH DIVIDE LIFE FROM Death are at best shadowy and vague," wrote Edgar Allan Poe in **"The Premature Burial**." "Who shall say where the one ends, and where the other begins?" Perhaps no "modern" fiction writer has explored the realm of dying, death, mourning, and burial with such dread as Poe, the American author known for his tales of the grim and ghastly. In 1845, Poe published his poem "The Raven," which described a supernatural visitation of a bird to a man mourning the loss of his love, Lenore. The poem brought Poe some fame but little money.

"The Raven" is filled will allusions to the afterlife. At one point, the narrator feels the presence of **angels** and wonders if God is sending some kind of sign. The narrator also suggests that the raven is "from the Night's Plutonian shore," referring to Pluto, another name for **Hades**, the ruler of the underworld in classical mythology.

Poe wrote in 1846, "The death . . . of a beautiful woman is, unquestionably, the most poetical topic in the world." Alas, Poe's own wife died of tuberculosis two years after the publication of his most famous poem. Written years earlier, his short tale "Ligeia" (1838) tells the story of a narrator's beautiful, intelligent raven-haired wife who dies and is later reanimated while the narrator keeps vigil over his second wife's dead body.

According to the English professor J. Gerald Kennedy, "While magazines and gift books purveyed sentimentalized images of death, Poe conjured subversive scenes of dissolution, dismemberment, and decomposition. His poems and tales defined a twilight zone of primal anxiety and endless melancholy." Although Poe's tales of death and dying are too numerous to describe here, consider "The Facts in the Case of M. Valdemar" (1845), in which the narrator describes a "true" story of a Mr. Valdemar who was hypnotized as he died and thus resides at the transition between life and death for months. Finally, the narrator attempts to awaken Valdemar and in the process triggers Valdemar's immediate decay. The story concludes, "Upon the bed, before that whole company, there lay a nearly liquid mass of loathsome—of detestable putridity."

See also Children and *Capacocha* (1622), Premature Burial (1844), Death's-Head Hawk Moth (1846), *The Death of Ivan Ilyich* (1886), Lovecraft's Reanimator (1922)

1845

A poster for a 1908 production of *The Raven: The Love Story of Edgar Allan Poe*, written by actor and playwright George Cochrane Hazelton, Jr. (1868–1921).

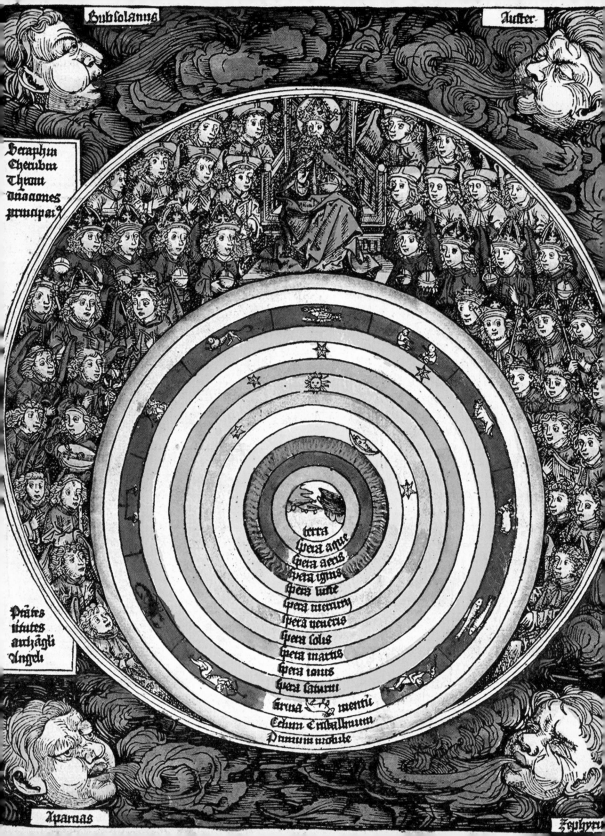

SUMMER LAND

EMANUEL SWEDENBORG (1688–1772), ANDREW JACKSON DAVIS (1826–1910)

ANDREW JACKSON DAVIS, THE "POUGHKEEPSIE seer," was a diviner and healer. His followers compared him to the Swedish scientist, Christian mystic, philosopher, and theologian Emanuel Swedenborg. In 1845, Davis coined the term "Summer Land" to designate the realm of the afterlife, which he said took the form of a series of spheres through which the spirit progressed after death. Spirits of the dead are drawn together on the basis of their commonality of emotions, moral conditions, and interests. By seeking spiritual knowledge, spirits could progress through the spheres, perfecting themselves and eventually approaching the sphere of the deity.

So far, no soul has gotten beyond the second sphere; however, someday, when all spirits ascend to the sixth sphere, God (who fills the seventh sphere) will create a new universe and a new set of spheres of spiritual existence. After this, the spirits in the sixth sphere will be in the new second sphere. Davis wrote, "The spirit will have no final home, because rest would be intolerable to an immortal being, but the spirit will progress eternally. It will be always in harmony with surrounding circumstances, and so will dwell always in heaven."

In *The Great Harmonia* (1852–1866), he clarified: "After the individual souls leave this planet . . . they ascend to the Second Sphere of existence. Here, *all* individuals undergo an angelic discipline, by which every physical and spiritual deformity is removed. . . . When all spirits shall have progressed to the Second Sphere, the various earths and planets in the Universe . . . will be depopulated, and not a living thing will move upon their surfaces."

In *A Stellar Key to the Summer Land* (1867) Davis writes: "According to my most careful examination of the physical structure of the Summer Land, the fertile soils, and the lovely groves and vines and flowers which infinitely diversify the landscape, are constituted of particles that were once in human bodies!" The Summer Land concept—which bears some resemblance to the Buddhist notion of **reincarnation** while hinting at the scientific idea of the nutrient cycle—was later used, with some variation, by Theosophists, Wiccans, and various modern pagan religions.

See also Heaven (c. 2400 BCE), The Elysian Fields (c. 850 BCE), Reincarnation (c. 600 BCE), Séance (1848)

For millennia, people have speculated about the physical structure of heaven and the afterlife. Andrew Jackson Davis's "Summer Land" involved a series of spheres that resembles this illustration of the biblical seventh day of creation from *The Nuremberg Chronicle* (1493) by German historian and physician Hartmann Schedel (1440–1514).

DEATH'S-HEAD HAWK MOTH

AGNES MURGOCI (1875–1929), EDGAR ALLAN POE (1809–1849),
MICHAEL MAJERUS (1954–2009)

WITH A WINGSPAN OF ABOUT 4 OR 5 INCHES (about 11.5 centimeters), the death's-head hawk moth has long been associated with death and other bad omens. For example, in 1926, the English zoologist and folklorist Dr. Agnes Murgoci wrote that in Romania, "it is thought that many people can project their soul as a butterfly. In Vâlcea, souls of **vampires** are considered to be incarnated in death's-head moths, which, when caught, should be impaled on a pin and stuck to a wall to prevent their flying further." In Bram Stoker's *Dracula*, the count sent those moths as food to Renfield, a madman with strange eating habits. In *The Silence of the Lambs*, the killer placed a pupa of this moth in the mouths of his victims. Even the master horror writer Edgar Allan Poe mentioned similar moths in his tale "The Sphinx" (1846), writing, "The Death's-headed Sphinx has occasioned much terror among the vulgar, at times, by the melancholy kind of cry which it utters, and the insignia of death which it wears upon its corslet."

The term *death's-head hawk moth* refers to several species of moth in the genus *Acherontia* that emit a loud, creepy squeak if irritated. The moths have a human-skull pattern on their backs, and their larvae will bite if threatened. They also raid beehives in a quest for honey. Interestingly, the three moth species names (*atropos, lachesis, styx*) are all from Greek myths and are related to death. Atropos was the goddess who ended lives by cutting our mortal threads, and her sister Lachesis determined our precise life spans. Styx is the famous river that divides the earth from the underworld, **Hades**.

More generally, through history, moths sometimes were seen as spirits. If a large moth was seen in the room of a dying person, it might have been viewed as the soul leaving the body. According to the British insect biologist Mike Majerus, "In Hungary . . . the entry of a Death's-head into a dwelling place is considered a harbinger of an imminent death in the family. In France, it was thought that a single scale from the wing of a Death's-head in one's eye would cause blindness."

See also Hades (c. 850 BCE), Grim Reaper (1424), Vampires (1819), Sin-Eaters (1825), "The Raven" (1845), *On Death and Dying* (1969)

An illustration of the death's-head hawk moth (*Acherontia atropos*) from a German reference work titled *Europe's Best-Known Butterflies* (1895). This moth has long been associated with death and other bad omens.

MISS MARGARETTA FOX.   MISS CATHARINE FOX.   MRS. FISH.

LITH. & PUB. BY N. CURRIER.   Entered according to Act of Congress in the year 1852 by N. Currier in the Clerks Office of the District Court of the Southern District of N.Y.   152 NASSAU ST. COR. OF SPRUCE. ST. N.Y.

SÉANCE

MARY TODD LINCOLN (1818-1882), ALFRED RUSSEL WALLACE (1823-1913), MARGARETTA
FOX (1833-1893), KATE FOX (1836-1892), ALEXANDER GRAHAM BELL (1847-1922),
GUGLIELMO MARCONI (1874-1937), HARRY HOUDINI (BORN ERIK WEISZ, 1874-1926)

ON DECEMBER 11, 1847, TEENAGE SISTERS KATE and Margaretta Fox moved with their parents into a house in Hydesville, New York. The house had a reputation for being haunted: there were several recorded instances of taps and other noises, and the prior tenant, Michael Weakman, allegedly had moved out of the house because of the strange disturbances. In March 1848, Margaretta and Kate claimed to hear mysterious noises. A supposed spirit—nicknamed "Mr. Splitfoot" (referring to the Devil) by the sisters—began communicating with them through rapping sounds (for example, one rap for "no" and two raps for "yes"). The rappings followed the sisters when they moved to Rochester, New York, and they began organizing "performances" in theaters to which they charged admission, attracting attention and skepticism. Eventually the sisters became the most famous mediums of nineteenth-century American spiritualism, a movement based on the idea that communication with spirits is possible that claimed about two million followers by 1855. In 1888, the sisters confessed to a newspaper reporter that the entire spirit-rapping phenomenon was an outright fraud. They gave a demonstration of how they were able to make the loud rapping noises by popping their toe and knee joints; not long afterward, they died in poverty.

A séance is an attempt to communicate with spirits, usually though a gathering of people who often were seated around a table in a darkened room. Spirits allegedly could communicate by speaking through mediums, automatic writing, and Ouija boards or by moving objects. Well-known séances include those arranged by Mary Todd Lincoln in 1863 at the White House while grieving over the loss of her and Abraham's son. Several famous scientists were attracted to the spiritualist ideas of contacting the dead, among them evolutionary biologist Alfred Russel Wallace, Guglielmo Marconi (a pioneer of radio transmission), and Alexander Graham Bell (inventor of the first practical telephone). Skeptics included the illusionist and stuntman Harry Houdini. Despite the long history of attempts to debunk fraudulent mediumship, séances are still performed.

See also The Witch of Endor (c. 1007 BCE), Necromancy (c. 850 BCE), Ghosts (c. 100 CE), Banshee (1350), Summer Land (1845), Searches for the Soul (1907), *The Grass Harp* (1951), Electronic Voice Phenomena (1956)

The Fox sisters: Margaretta (left) and Kate (center), with older sister Leah Fox Fish (1814-1890, right). The two younger sisters seemed to convince Leah that they were communicating with spirits, and Leah began to manage their careers.

1848

OPHELIA

WILLIAM SHAKESPEARE (1564-1616), JOHN EVERETT MILLAIS (1829-1896),
ELIZABETH ELEANOR SIDDAL (1829-1862), SALVADOR DALÍ (1904-1989)

OPHELIA (1852) BY ENGLISH PAINTER JOHN Millais—a poignant and detailed painting that represents a person at the threshold of death—is one of the most famous depictions of female **suicide**. Ophelia, a potential wife of Prince Hamlet in William Shakespeare's play *Hamlet*, goes mad and finally drowns herself in one of the most poetically described death scenes in literature when she climbs a willow tree while gathering flowers, the branch breaks, and she falls into a brook. Once in the water, she floats for a while, "her clothes spread wide, and mermaid-like a while they bore her up." She does not seem to realize or care that death is imminent, and as her dress becomes heavy with water, she is pulled beneath the surface "to muddy death."

Before painting the dying girl, Millais took great care in painting a botanically lush background that nearly overwhelms the scene with its verdant complexity. He sometimes spent as many as eleven hours a day over several months painting outdoors along the banks of the Hogsmill River in England. To represent Ophelia—and her melding of innocence and insanity—Millais had nineteen-year-old Elizabeth Siddal lie fully clothed in a bathtub in his studio, with oil lamps placed underneath the tub for warmth. Ironically, in 1862 Siddal overdosed on laudanum in what may have been an act of suicide at the age of thirty-two.

The surrealist painter Salvador Dalí said the painting showed a "radiant" woman who is both "the most desirable and most frightening." Educator Ron Brown wrote, "Her garments resemble the bright colours of a dragonfly. Like a bright-coloured stain on the water, watery against the water, a flower against the flowers, 'Ophelia' mimics the background and fuses with nature." English professor Julia Thomas notes that beyond their "botanical fidelity," the plants have a symbolic status. "The poppy at Ophelia's right hand signifies death, the daisies are symbolic of innocence, roses of youth, pansies of unrequited love, the fritillary floating in the stream at the bottom right of the painting symbolizes sorrow, and the violets that hang around Ophelia's neck represent faithfulness."

See also Suicide (c. 300 BCE), Death Mask (c. 1888), Crucifixion Vision of Tissot (c. 1890), Schwabe's *The Death of the Gravedigger* (1895), *The Garden of Death* (1896), *The Wounded Angel* (1903), Kamikaze Pilots (1944), *The Grass Harp* (1951)

Ophelia **(oil on canvas)** by John Everett Millais.

EMBALMING

ALEXANDER III OF MACEDON (356–323 BCE), HORATIO NELSON (1758–1805),
ABRAHAM LINCOLN (1809–1865), AUGUST WILHELM VON HOFMANN (1818–1892)

MBALMING, THE ART AND SCIENCE OF PRES-erving human remains to hinder decomposition and create aesthetic presentations, has had a long history (see the entry on **Mummies**). For example, the ancient inhabitants of Egypt, Ecuador, Peru, and the Canary Islands practiced some form of the art. The ancient Greeks perfumed and spiced the dead. The ancient Scythians of central Eurasia disemboweled their rulers and filled their bodies with anise, cypress, and frankincense before covering the bodies in wax. The corpse of Alexander the Great probably was persevered in honey and wax for its long journey to Memphis, Egypt. In 1805, the body of British admiral Horatio Nelson was returned to London in a barrel of brandy.

Embalming became more common in the United States during the Civil War with the return of dead soldiers to their faraway families. The embalming of President Abraham Lincoln's body to facilitate its long tour and viewing through the United States also made embalming more familiar to everyday citizens.

In 1867, German chemist August Wilhelm von Hofmann synthesized formaldehyde, a chemical soon discovered to be useful for corpse preservation, gradually replacing previous approaches using alcohol, mercury, and arsenic. Today, arterial embalming (with formaldehyde mixed with other chemicals) is performed by injecting embalming chemicals into blood vessels, especially the right common carotid artery. Blood and other fluids are displaced and drained from the right jugular vein. The contents of other cavities are replaced by using trocars that pierce the body.

Although Muslims and religious Jews typically do not make use of embalming, religious scholar Gary Laderman notes, "Embalming was the lifeblood of the American funeral industry from the beginning of the twentieth century. [Soon] Americans no longer died in the familiar surrounding of the home, but in the . . . frequently inaccessible space of the hospital, where another class of specialists cared for the body not yet dead. Finally, in the midst of the fast-paced technologically driven changes in modern society, more and more Americans continued to long for a fixed, permanent image of the deceased at peace."

See also Cremation (c. 20,000 BCE), Mummies (c. 5050 BCE), Funeral Processions (c. 1590), Autopsy (1761), Cryonics (1962)

This center oak panel (oil and gold leaf, c. 1410) from a triptych painted in Bruges, Belgium, shows the embalming of the body of Jesus. The artist is unknown.

EUHANASIA

JACOB "JACK" KEVORKIAN (1928–2011)

"EVERY DAY, RATIONAL PEOPLE ALL OVER THE world plead to be allowed to die," writes the lawyer Ronald Dworkin. "Sometimes they plead for others to kill them. Some of them are dying already. . . . Some of them want to die because they are unwilling to live in the only way left open to them." The term *euthanasia* usually refers to the intentional ending of someone's life to relieve suffering and pain such as that caused by an incurable disease or to the killing of someone in an irreversible coma. *Active euthanasia* involves the administration of lethal substances or forces, and *passive euthanasia* entails the withholding of treatments. *Voluntary euthanasia* is conducted with the consent of the patient. Active voluntary euthanasia is legal in some European countries, and passive voluntary euthanasia is legal throughout the United States. When patients are provided the means for and killing themselves, this is referred to as *assisted* **suicide.**

Euthanasia has been practiced since ancient times in a variety of cultures, although it usually was opposed in Judeo-Christian traditions, which punished it by leaving the bodies of suicides at the side of a road or impaled on a stake or by denying family members inheritances. The pre-Christian Roman colony of Massalia (present-day Marseille), in contrast, took a pragmatic approach, allowing citizens to apply to the senate for free hemlock to carry out the deed but denying soldiers and slaves the same right for economic reasons.

One famous event in the history of euthanasia involves the publication of an influential 1872 essay in England on the subject by schoolteacher Samuel D. Williams, who wrote, "In all cases of hopeless and painful illness, it should be the recognized duty of the medical attendant, whenever so desired by the patient, to administer chloroform or such other anesthetic . . . to put the sufferer to a quick and painless death. The remedy [should be] applied at the express wish of the patient."

Assisted suicide has been legal in Switzerland since the 1940s, and it has been more recently legalized in the Netherlands, Luxembourg, Belgium, and some U.S. states. The recent rise in the number of people who are terminally ill—including people with neurological conditions such as paralysis, amyotrophic lateral sclerosis, Parkinson's disease, and multiple sclerosis—traveling abroad to places such as Switzerland to end their lives has sparked controversy and debate about "right to die laws" in many countries.

See also Suicide (c. 300 BCE), Abortion (c. 70 CE), Black Death (1347), Hospice (1967), Brain Death (1968), Do Not Resuscitate (1976)

A molecule of morphine ($C_{17}H_{19}NO_3$). In the mid-1800s, morphine began to be used increasingly to ease the deaths of people in pain. Its use was promoted by American surgeon John Warren (1778–1856).

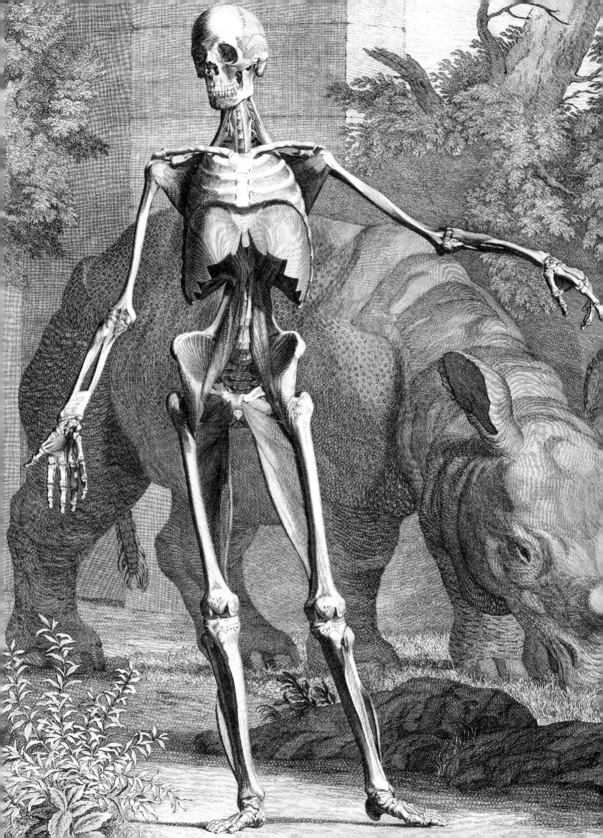

WALKING CORPSE SYNDROME

JULES COTARD (1840–1889)

"I USED TO HAVE A HEART," SAID A PATIENT WITH THE walking corpse syndrome. "I have something which beats in its place. . . . I have no stomach. I never feel hungry. When I eat . . . it seems that food falls into a hole." This rare mental disorder is also called Cotard's syndrome (CS) after the French neurologist Jules Cotard, who described the disorder in 1880. People with CS mistakenly believe that they have lost organs or that they have died and are animated corpses. They sometimes believe that their brains, stomachs, intestines, hearts, blood, or spirits are missing. Those afflicted also may feel damned and think that their bodies have been reduced to machines. Paradoxically, these "walking corpses" also may say that they are immortal. Psychiatrists David Enoch and Hadrian Ball write, "This, then, becomes the greatest despair of all—wishing to [die] but condemned to live forever in the state of nihilism, a state reminiscent of Kierkegaard's living **hell**."

CS may result from a disconnect between the brain area that recognizes faces (the fusiform area) and the regions that associate emotion with faces (e.g., the amygdala). It may be triggered by head injury, brain tumors, brain atrophy, seizure disorders, typhoid fever, and the antiviral drug acyclovir. Some brain scans show extremely low metabolic activity across large areas of the frontal and parietal brain regions in CS patients. Treatments include electroconvulsive therapy, antidepressants, and antipsychotics.

Some people with CS also deny the existence of the external world and refuse to eat or drink. There are chilling accounts of such individuals wanting to spend time in graveyards, morgues, or coffins. CS bears some similarity to psychiatric disorders such as Capgras syndrome, in which individuals may believe that family members have been replaced by "doubles" or "imposters." Similarly, Odysseus syndrome ("nihilism by proxy") is the delusional belief that loved ones have died or that their body parts or organs have been replaced or are putrefying despite evidence to the contrary.

See also Golem (1580), "The Monkey's Paw" (1902), Searches for the Soul (1907), Zombies (1968), *On Death and Dying* (1969)

People with CS believe that they have lost organs or are animated corpses. Shown here is a walking corpse with missing viscera from *Tabulae sceleti et musculorum corporis humani* (1749: Tables of the skeleton and muscles of the human body) by German-born anatomist Bernhard Siegfried Albinus (1697–1770).

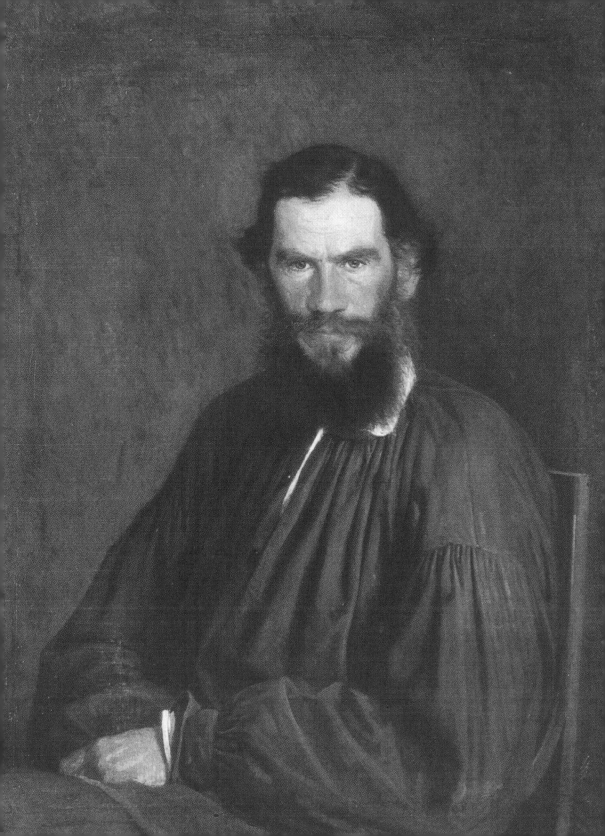

THE DEATH OF IVAN ILYICH

LEV NIKOLAYEVICH TOLSTOY (1828–1910)

THE DEATH OF IVAN ILYICH (1886) IS A NOVELLA by Russian writer Leo Tolstoy, who is well known for his monumental novels *War and Peace* (1869) and *Anna Karenina* (1877). The story was written shortly after Tolstoy's embrace of a radical anarcho-pacifist Christian philosophy and reflects his overwhelming concern about the inevitability of death. Ilyich, the main character, is a judge who seeks career advancement and a routine life more than emotional involvement with his family. Within weeks of injuring the side of his body while hanging curtains in his new apartment, he experiences a strange taste in his mouth and increasing pain. He consults physicians, who can do nothing for him. In the end, he spends three days screaming in horror and pain.

Interestingly, the novella begins with Ilyich's funeral, thus introducing the reader to a man who already has died. Then a kind of space-time warping is used by Tolstoy in showing the life of Ilyich. The first four chapters span more than forty years. The second four chapters cover only a few months, and the final four chapters span roughly four weeks. Spatial contraction is also evident, as Ilyich's early life is spent moving among towns. Subsequently, he settles in a single city. When he becomes sick, he stays in his study, and near the end of the novel, he essentially is confined to his sofa.

As his life slips away, Ilyich finally feels empathy for those he is leaving behind and hopes that his death will release them. He hears someone near him say, "He's gone." Ilyich tells himself, "Death has gone," and then draws his last breath. According to English author Ronald Blythe, "Tolstoy raises up this dull and rather despicable man until something about him shines sufficiently for the reader to catch a glimpse of himself. . . . When pain is searching out the breaking point of the intellect, another factor, call it the soul or spirit or the true self, emerges."

See also "The Raven" (1845), *Ophelia* (1852), Last Words of the Dying (1922), Golding's Liminal World (1956), Hospice (1967), *On Death and Dying* (1969)

This portrait of Leo Tolstoy as a young man was painted in 1873 by Ivan Nikolaevich Kramskoi (1837–1887).

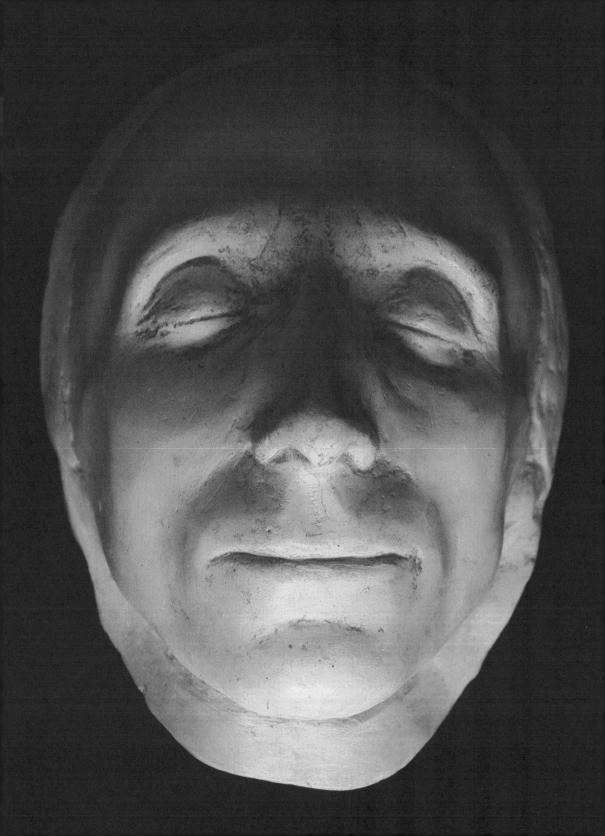

DEATH MASK

"ALTHOUGH THE EYES ARE SAID TO BE THE windows of the soul," writes author Christine Quigley, "when they are closed to death the entire face becomes a mirror of the life it once housed. Preserving its image has been a sacred duty over the centuries." A death mask is generally a three-dimensional representation of a person's face after death, made of wax, plaster, or some other substance. For example, a traditional death mask might be made by placing oil on the face and then pouring plaster to make a mold.

These masks have served many different purposes through time. Sometimes they have been displayed at state funerals, used to identify a person before the invention of photography, displayed in museums as items of curiosity, or employed for the purposes of medical study. In the past, the death masks of executed criminals often were examined for possible evidence of or clues to psychopathic inclinations based on the appearance and structure of the face.

Many death masks have been made for famous people, including musical giants Ludwig van Beethoven and Frédéric Chopin; the national leaders Napoleon Bonaparte, Abraham Lincoln, and Henry VIII; and poet Dante Alighieri. Other "masked greats" include Benjamin Franklin, Alfred Hitchcock, Woodrow Wilson, Nikola Tesla, and Isaac Newton. One of the most famous death masks in history is that of an unidentified young woman (c. 1888) with a slight smile who, around age sixteen, was found drowned in the Seine River in Paris. Referred to as *L'Inconnue de la Seine* ("the unknown woman of the Seine"), she became the inspiration for many literary works, and replicas of her mask were frequently displayed on the walls of artists and other curious people.

Ernst Benkard wrote in his 1929 book *Undying Faces*, "Because the death mask stands and admonishes us at the gateway between what we call life and what we call death, it will always bear a supernatural character, as something which cannot be gauged by our experience of sunrise, night, and another day. It is the last symbol of a man, his undying face."

See also Mummies (c. 5050 BCE), Epitaphs (c. 480 BCE), *Ophelia* (1852)

Death mask of the Italian saint Vincent Pallotti (1795–1850), who helped the poor in Rome. When his body was exhumed in 1906 and 1950, it was found to be incorrupt (a sign of holiness), and it now can be viewed, fully intact, at the church of San Salvatore in Onda.

CRUCIFIXION VISION OF TISSOT

JAMES JACQUES JOSEPH TISSOT (1836–1902)

THE PAINTING FREQUENTLY KNOWN AS *WHAT Our Lord Saw from the Cross* (c. 1890) by French painter James Tissot is special in that we see the artist's vision of what Jesus might have seen as he gazed down during his crucifixion. The curators at the Brooklyn Museum note, "Ultimately, the image is an exercise in empathy. Its point is to give viewers, accustomed to looking at the event from the outside, a rare opportunity to imagine themselves in Christ's place and consider his final thoughts and feelings as he gazed on the enemies and friends who were witnessing, or participating in, his death."

Tissot's mother was a devout Roman Catholic, and in 1885 he experienced a renewed interest in Catholicism that led him to spend the rest of his life illustrating the Bible. To help him make these illustrations, Tissot traveled to the Middle East to study the landscapes, architectures, and people. His series of 365 gouache (opaque watercolor) paintings illustrating the life of Christ received critical acclaim in New York, Paris, and London. His biographer Krystyna Matyjaszkiewicz wrote of his religious passion:

Tissot set off for Palestine on 15 October 1886, his fiftieth birthday. He returned to Paris in March 1887 with sketchbooks full of drawings and a burning compulsion to illustrate the life of Christ. [He published] images of events, places, people, and incidental detail, with extracts from the Gospels and biblical commentaries. Tissot made further visits to Jerusalem, [and] by April 1894 he had completed 270 watercolors, which were displayed at the Champ de Mars, Paris, to awe and amazement. . . .

If we study the painting shown here, we see Mary Magdalene in the immediate foreground at the bottom, with long red hair, next to a glimpse of Jesus's feet. Farther back, Tissot shows the Virgin Mary clutching her breast. A Roman centurion looks on from the left, and Jewish leaders stare from the back and the right. Tissot also depicts an entrance to a tomb for Jesus's body toward the back of the painting.

See also Capital Punishment (c. 1772 BCE), Resurrection (c. 30 CE), *The Wounded Angel* (1903), Thanatourism (1996)

C. 1890

What Our Lord Saw from the Cross by James Tissot (opaque watercolor over graphite on gray-green wove paper). Mary Magdalene, with long red hair, is in the immediate foreground at the bottom, next to a glimpse of Jesus's feet.

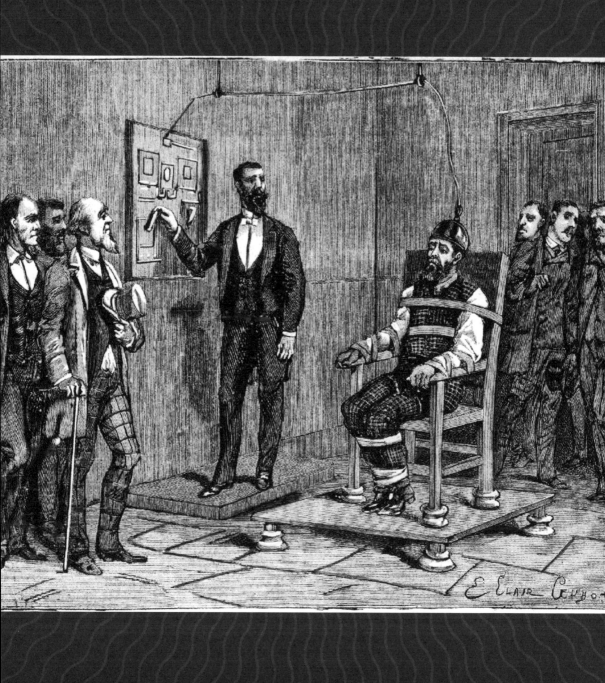

ELECTRIC CHAIR

GEORGE WESTINGHOUSE, JR. (1846–1914), THOMAS ALVA EDISON (1847–1931), MARTHA M. PLACE (1849–1899), HAROLD PITNEY BROWN (1857–1944), WILLIAM FRANCIS KEMMLER (1860–1890), ARTHUR EDWIN KENNELLY (1861–1939)

+ ☠ +

ON AUGUST 6, 1890, WILLIAM KEMMLER BECAME the first person to be executed in an electric chair. Early that morning, he dressed in a suit and tie, had breakfast, and said some prayers. At around 6:30 a.m., Kemmler entered the execution room, saying, "Gentlemen, I wish you all good luck. I believe I am going to a good place, and I am ready to go." The electric chair had been developed recently as a more humane alternative to hanging.

The generator was charged with 1,000 volts and applied for seventeen seconds, yet Kemmler still lived, and so 2,000 volts was applied. The *New York Times* reported that "an awful odor began to permeate the death chamber . . . and the hair under and around the electrode on the head and the flesh under and around the electrode at the base of the spine was singeing." A reporter who witnessed the electrocution said it was "an awful spectacle, far worse than hanging." George Westinghouse, the American pioneer of the electrical industry, commented, "They would have done better using an axe." In a later execution, a man was "electrocuted," only to be later observed breathing in the autopsy room. Incidents exist in which a person's head caught on fire.

The electric chair was invented by Harold P. Brown and Arthur Kennelly, both of whom worked for inventor Thomas Edison, who was a proponent of DC (direct current) electricity at that time. Partly to demonstrate the danger of the competing AC (alternating current) electrical standards, Edison chose AC for the electric chair, and Brown and Edison publicly killed many animals with AC to show its lethality.

The first woman to be executed by electrocution was Mrs. Martha Place in 1899. Although the electric chair was once the most common execution method in the United States—with 4,251 such executions between 1890 and 1972—today lethal injection (usually a fatal dose of a barbiturate, a paralytic, and a potassium solution) has widely taken its place.

See also Capital Punishment (c. 1772 BCE), Suicide (c. 300 BCE), Guillotine (1792), *Frankenstein* (1818), Quantum Immortality (1987)

This depiction of the execution of William Kemmler on August 6, 1890, appeared in the prominent French newspaper *Le Petit Parisien.*

GHOST DANCE

SITTING BULL (C. 1831–1890), WOVOKA, AKA JACK WILSON (C. 1856–1932)

IMAGINE LIVING AS A NATIVE AMERICAN IN THE western United States around 1890, having suffered the ruin of your culture, defeat in war, starvation, disease, and confinement to federally designated tribal lands. Some Native Americans were expected to send their children to boarding schools that were forbidden to teach Native American traditional culture and language. In such a dire situation, what teachings might you accept to lift your spirits?

The Ghost Dance was part of a religious movement promoted by Wovoka, the Northern Paiute prophet from Nevada also known as Jack Wilson. While experiencing a vision during a solar eclipse on January 1, 1899, Wovoka said he died and was told by God to teach Native Americans a new dance that, along with proper behavior, would bring about the renewal of the world, including reunion with the Native American dead. The Ghost Dance was derived from the round dance, in which a circle of dancers proceed in a clockwise direction to singing drummers for hours, with some of the dancers in trancelike states. Wovoka told his people to love one another and live in peace with the whites. He foretold a land filled with wild game where hunger and disease would be no more. If people performed the five-day Ghost Dance at the appropriate intervals, it would hasten this era of harmony.

The message of the Ghost Dance spread across much of the western United States, with the Lakota Sioux people of the Great Plains emphasizing that the dance would bring about the removal of whites from their lands. Some Native Americans believed that "Ghost shirts" might repel bullets. The Ghost Dance movement scared many whites, eventually leading to the 1890 massacre that left at least 153 Sioux dead, many of whom were women and children, near Wounded Knee Creek in South Dakota. The Lakota chief Sitting Bull was killed by authorities while they tried to arrest him, fearing that he would join the Ghost Dance movement.

See also Heaven (c. 2400 BCE), The Elysian Fields (c. 850 BCE), Day of the Dead (1519), Children and *Capacocha* (1622), Summer Land (1845)

This illustration of the Sioux ghost dance appeared in the *London News* (1891) and also in *Recent Indian Wars under the Lead of Sitting Bull, and Other Chiefs* (1891) by James P. Boyd.

SCHWABE'S THE DEATH OF THE GRAVEDIGGER

CARLOS SCHWABE (1866-1926)

EATH HAS BEEN REPRESENTED AS AN UNEAR-thly entity in many civilizations, with personifications ranging from the skeletal **Grim Reaper** that appeared in the 1400s and earlier to the winged **Thanatos** of the ancient Greeks. In Hindu scriptures, the lord of death is **Yama**, who rides a black buffalo and carries rope to bring souls to the underworld, Naraka. In the West, one particularly famous depiction appears in *La mort du fossoyeur (The Death of the Gravedigger*, 1895) by German Symbolist painter Carlos Schwabe. Symbolism in the arts was a late nineteenth-century movement that emphasized dreams, fantasy, imagination, mythology, and spirituality.

In the painting, the angel of death is illuminated by the mysterious green light of a candle as she beckons heavenward. The **gravedigger** moves his hand toward his heart and lets go of his shovel. Nearby signs of life in the form of small flower buds are emerging from the snow-covered ground. Descending from above are the mostly bare tendrils of a tree, and in the background the snow appears pristine and untouched, blanketing the quiet, still, grizzled, but enduring headstones behind the angel.

In symbolist artworks, female figures sometimes represent creativity, suffering, or death. Interestingly, Schwabe's first wife was a model for his angels, including the female figure in *The Death of the Gravedigger*. When a close friend of Schwabe's died in 1894, his interest in death and dying intensified. Karl S. Guthke writes of Schwabe's angel of death: "The ends of her wings, soon to soar upward, reach into the open grave. Even the choice of colors accentuates this paradoxical ensemble of death and life: nature from which man is to be released is painted wintery white; the angel of death is garbed in the rich green of life."

See also Yama (c. 1100 BCE), Thanatos (c. 700 BCE), Angels (c. 380), Grim Reaper (1424), Gravediggers (1651), *Ophelia* (1852)

Schwabe's first wife served as the model for the death angel in *The Death of the Gravedigger*.

THE GARDEN OF DEATH

HUGO GERHARD SIMBERG (1873-1917)

THE GARDEN OF DEATH (1896) IS A PAINTING BY Finnish painter Hugo Simberg, who is famous for his depictions of death and the supernatural. In this renowned painting, the viewer sees three skeletons tending flowers in pots—an eerily comical and macabre depiction, especially given the central skeleton that appears to be smiling as he grasps a flower in front of where his heart would be. Is the skeletal being trying to suggest that death need not be so sad? Another unusual juxtaposition is the obvious pairing of flowers (symbols of life) with black-clad skeletons (symbols of death). Simberg usually did not offer explanations for his paintings, preferring to let viewers interpret the paintings for themselves, but he did describe this particular garden as the place where the dead go before ascending to **heaven**.

Several additional analyses have been offered over the years. For example, the image may suggest to the viewer that death and life are inextricably bound—one is not possible without the other. The painting also suggests that otherworldly transition realms may exist at the fuzzy boundaries of life and death.

Thatanology professor Sandra L. Bertman writes, "This artwork invites the viewer to consider the afterlife, to take comfort in his or her own passing, and to not fear what happens after the body fails to function."

If you look closely, you will notice that the flowers are not like any flowers typically found on Earth. Some resemble spiky eight-pointed and five-pointed stars, and others look like dark balls atop sinuous stems. Some flowers are white, and others are black. If the flowers represent the souls of people, the garden may be viewed as a kind of purgatory where souls might seek sustenance and nourishment before embarking on the final journey. Although the painting is rendered with flatness and simplicity, the viewer notes a path that leads away in the distance. Is it a route of entry to or exit from the cryptic garden?

See also Heaven (c. 2400 BCE), *The Epic of Gilgamesh* (c. 2000 BCE), Four Horsemen of the Apocalypse (c. 70 CE), Grim Reaper (1424), *Death and the Miser* (c. 1490), Day of the Dead (1519), *The Wounded Angel* (1903)

The Garden of Death (watercolor and gouache) by Hugo Simberg.

"THE MONKEY'S PAW"

WILLIAM WYMARK JACOBS (1863–1943)

"THE MONKEY'S PAW," A FRIGHTENING STORY by English author W. W. Jacobs, has been adapted in numerous plays, movies, television shows, and operas. With its chilling take on the transcendent themes of death, dread, and reanimation, the story has been included in over seventy fiction anthologies, parodied on *The Simpsons* on television, and served as a stimulus for the novels of Stephen King.

In the story, first published in 1902, Mr. and Mrs. White are given a monkey's paw that can grant three wishes. When Mr. White requests £200 so that he can make the final payment on his home, factory officials soon arrive at his home and pay him £200 as compensation for the sudden gruesome death of the couple's beloved son, Herbert, who was mangled in factory machinery, a detail that perhaps reminds the reader of the potential torture the dismembered monkey might have experienced.

Grieving after the son's burial, the couple decides to wish again—this time for Herbert to be alive and to return home. Alas, when there is a knock on the door later on, Mr. White fully realizes that the mutilated body of their son is probably waiting outside, and his fear escalates.

"For God's sake, don't let it in," Mr. White cries, but his wife ignores him and begins to open the front door to the home.

"You're afraid of your own son," she cries, struggling. A "fusillade" of knocks from outside reverberates through the house as Mr. White suddenly finds the paw and frantically breathes his third and final wish. The knocking suddenly ceases, leaving only echoes in the house. The door opens. A cold wind rushes in, and Mrs. White erupts in a long loud wail of disappointment and misery. Mr. White runs to her side, and outside all he sees is the street lamp flickering on a quiet and deserted road.

Like the classic Greek tragedy *Oedipus Rex,* the story of the supernatural monkey's paw warns readers that attempting to meddle with fate will do them no good. Writing about "The Monkey's Paw," philosopher Nicholas Rescher notes that we can never be sure "about our ability to tinker with reality to effect improvements in the world by somehow removing . . . imperfections through well-intentioned readjustments." How can we ever know if repairs to the fabric of reality will produce better results in the long run?

See also Resurrection (c. 30 CE), Resurrectionists (1832), Lovecraft's Reanimator (1922), *The Grass Harp* (1951), Zombies (1968)

In "The Monkey's Paw," a frightening story by English author W. W. Jacobs, Mr. and Mrs. White are given a monkey's paw that can grant three wishes.

THE WOUNDED ANGEL

HUGO GERHARD SIMBERG (1873–1917), RAINER MARIA RILKE (1875–1926)

N 1923, BOHEMIAN-AUSTRIAN POET RAINER MARIA Rilke published his *Duino Elegies*: intense, mystical poems that convey both beauty and suffering. His first elegy starts with a focus on **angels**:

Who, if I cried out, would hear me among the angels' hierarchies? And even if one of them pressed me suddenly against his heart: I would be consumed in that overwhelming existence. For beauty is nothing but the beginning of terror, which we still are just able to endure, and we are so awed because it serenely disdains to annihilate us. Every angel is terrifying. [Stephen Mitchell trans.]

Rilke's works are a meditation on life and death, the spiritual and the earthly, and humanity's contact with profound beauty. Other artists have depicted angels from complementary perspectives, and among the most perplexing of these alternative visions is that of the Finnish painter Hugo Simberg, who was born two years before Rilke. Simberg's painting The *Wounded Angel* (1903) shows an angel with a bloodied wing and bandaged eyes being carried on a stretcher. Her head is bowed, and she holds small white flowers. The landscape is subdued and bleak. The whiteness of her wings provides a stark contrast with the dark clothing of the two somber young boys carrying her. One of the boys looks toward the viewer. What are his emotions? Is he angry at humanity for some wrong done to the angel? Is he carrying her to a place where she can receive help? What exactly has been done to the angel? Could the boys have harmed her in some way? The meaning is in the eye of the beholder.

The landscape in this fascinating and famous painting is from Eläintarha (a park in Helsinki, Finland), and the water in the background is Töölönlahti Bay. The path upon which the boys walk still exists along the shore. Simberg never revealed to the public the intended meaning of the painting, wanting viewers to bring their own emotions and interpretations to the work. What do you see?

Interestingly, both Simberg and Rilke were "wounded" in their own ways, and that probably influenced their art. Simberg was recovering from meningitis right before he finished his painting, and Rilke's poems were seeded during and after a bout of severe depression.

See also Angels (c. 380), *Jacob's Dream* (c. 1805), Crucifixion Vision of Tissot (c. 1890), *The Garden of Death* (1896)

The Wounded Angel (oil on canvas) by Hugo Simberg.

SEARCHES FOR THE SOUL

HEROPHILUS (335–280 BCE), RENÉ DESCARTES (1596–1650),
DUNCAN MACDOUGALL (1866–1920)

VARIOUS FUTURISTS HAVE SUGGESTED THAT AS we learn more about the structure of the brain, technologists one day may be able to simulate a mind or upload it to a computer. These speculations assume a *materialist* view in which the mind arises from brain activity. In constrast, many thinkers adhere to the philosophy of mind-body *dualism* in which the soul and matter are seen as separate entities. The French philosopher René Descartes in the mid-1600s supposed that the mind, or "soul," exists separately from the brain but is connected via the pineal body, which he called "the seat of the soul." The ancient Greek physician Herophilus dissected heads and decided that the soul was situated in the fluid-filled calamus scriptorius, a cavity in the floor of the fourth cerebral ventricle of the brain.

In 1907, American physician Duncan MacDougall placed six dying tuberculosis patients on scales. He reasoned that at the moment of death, the scales should indicate a drop in weight as the soul left. As a result of his experiments, MacDougall measured the soul to be 21 grams (0.7 ounces). Alas, he and other researchers never were able to duplicate this finding.

A more materialist view of the mind and body may be supported by experiments that suggest that thoughts, memory, and personality can be altered by damage to regions of the brain and that brain imaging studies can map both feelings and thoughts. As just one curious example, injury to the brain's right frontal lobe can lead to a sudden, passionate interest in fine restaurants and gourmet foods—a condition called *gourmand syndrome*. Of course, the dualist Descartes might have argued that damage to the brain alters behavior because it is through the brain that the mind operates. If we excise the car's steering wheel, the car behaves differently, but this does not necessarily mean that there is no driver.

See also Séance (1848), Electronic Voice Phenomena (1956), Cryonics (1962), Brain Death (1968), *On Death and Dying* (1969), Near-Death Experiences (1975)

The Death of a Bishop (tempera on gold-ground panel) by an anonymous fifteenth-century Catalan artist. An angel and a devil are depicted at the top of the painting, fighting over the departing soul of the dying bishop.

LAST WORDS OF THE DYING

ROBERT ERSKINE CHILDERS (1870-1922), LENA BAKER (1901-1945),
TIMOTHY FRANCIS LEARY (1920-1996), STEVEN PAUL JOBS (1955-2011)

"THE LAST WORDS OF THE DYING ARE LIKE THE final line of a haiku or the clue hidden among the inscrutable folds of a Zen koan," writes author Alan Bisbort. "The only one thing one can say with certainty about them is that all that follows in their wake is the infinite silence, the mystery of death. . . . The dead have their say, and we the living are left to ponder what their words could mean." (Of course, it is possible that some last words mean little and are the scattered effluvia of a dying mind.)

Last words come in many forms. Some are part of a formal statement, such as that expressed by a person about to be executed for a crime. Erskine Childers, the Irish nationalist and gun smuggler, spoke these bold words to the firing squad just before his execution in 1922: "Take a step or two forward, lads. It will be easier that way." Lena Baker, an African American maid and mother of three children and the only woman to be executed by electrocution in Georgia, had been threatened by her employer with an iron bar and had immediately reported her shooting of him to the authorities. Unlike Childers, she sought to clear her name moments before her electrocution in 1945: "What I done, I did in self-defense, or I would have been killed myself. . . . I am ready to meet my God. I have a very strong conscience."

Other, less deliberate final phrases uttered as death approaches are more cryptic. The last words of American psychologist Timothy Leary, a champion of psychedelic drugs, were "Why not?" repeatedly uttered in different intonations, and finally, "Beautiful." Computer pioneer Steve Jobs mysteriously observed, "Oh wow. Oh wow. Oh wow." Although this was by no means a scientific survey, some hospice nurses who observed thousands of deaths noted certain potential commonalities in last words. For example, American hospice nurse Maggie Callanan suggested that the dying often use travel metaphors for death and talk about having to get ready for a trip.

See also Epitaphs (480 BCE), Martyr (c. 135), Obituaries (1731), *The Death of Ivan Ilyich* (1886), Kamikaze Pilots (1944), *On Death and Dying* (1969)

After writing a "death poem," General Akashi Gidayu prepares to commit seppuku (ritual suicide) after losing a battle in 1582. Japanese artist Yoshitoshi Tsukioka (1839–1892) created this artwork around 1890.

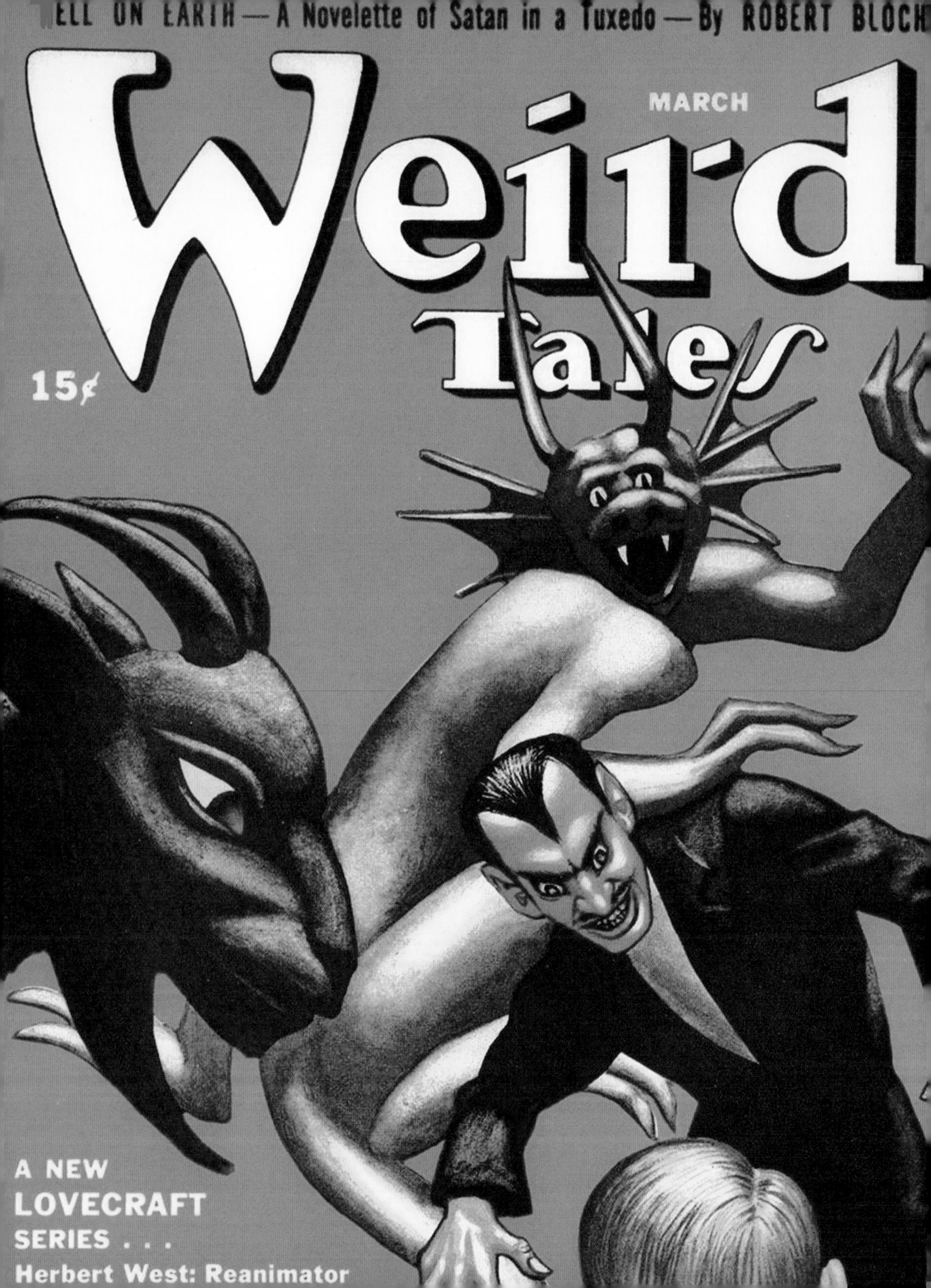
HELL ON EARTH—A Novelette of Satan in a Tuxedo—By ROBERT BLOCH
Weird Tales
MARCH
15¢
A NEW
LOVECRAFT
SERIES . . .
Herbert West: Reanimator

LOVECRAFT'S REANIMATOR

HOWARD PHILLIPS LOVECRAFT (1890-1937), DAVID PAUL CRONENBERG (B. 1943), STEPHEN EDWIN KING (B. 1947), JOHN HOWARD CARPENTER (B. 1948)

"IT'S OFTEN BEEN SAID THAT READING HORROR fiction is a way of rehearsing death, of flirting with our own mortality without going all the way," writes American novelist Poppy Brite. "[Perhaps] H. P. Lovecraft owes some of his posthumous popularity to a shell-shocked post–World War II readership trying to come to terms with the fact that the universe just didn't care about humanity...."

American author H. P. Lovecraft is one of the most influential horror writers of all time, with strong influences on a host of luminaries, such as novelist Stephen King and filmmakers John Carpenter and David Cronenberg. His story "Herbert West—Reanimator" (1922) is famous for depicting zombielike beings that are scientifically reanimated and was also the basis for the 1985 cult horror film *Re-Animator*.

In Lovecraft's tale, we learn that the brilliant, narcissistic Herbert West, while still in college, began "his terrible experiments, first on small animals and then on human bodies shockingly obtained. There was a solution which he injected into the veins of dead things, and if they were fresh enough they responded in strange ways." West's failed experiments produced "nameless things resulting from imperfect solutions or from bodies insufficiently fresh." At the end of the tale, West meets his demise when zombielike beings attack. "I saw outlined against some phosphorescence of the nether world a horde of silent toiling things which only insanity—or worse—could create. Their outlines were human, semi-human, fractionally human, and not human at all—the horde was grotesquely heterogeneous."

A large proportion of Lovecraft's collection of weird fiction journeys into the deepest recesses of cosmic horror. American novelist Barbara Hambly writes, "Lovecraft was a man with a vision of the world: astonishing, macabre, intricate as a Giger drawing. His sense of cosmoses opening out of cosmoses, of dark abysses concealing in their hearts the entrances to further gulfs, infuses nearly everything he wrote with an atmosphere, not of horror, but of wonder."

See also Golem (1580), *Frankenstein* (1818), Resurrectionists (1832), "The Raven" (1845), Walking Corpse Syndrome (1880), "The Monkey's Paw" (1902), Brain Death (1968), Zombies (1968)

Cover of the magazine *Weird Tales* (March 1942, vol. 36, no. 4) featuring *Herbert West: Reanimator* by H.P. Lovecraft. The art is by Hannes Bok, a pseudonym for Wayne Woodard (1914-1964).

GENOCIDE

RAPHAEL LEMKIN (1900–1959), ALAIN DESTEXHE (B. 1958)

ALTHOUGH GENOCIDE PROBABLY HAS BEEN practiced since the dawn of humanity, the word was not coined until 1944, when Polish-Jewish lawyer Raphael Lemkin created it from the Greek *genos* ("race" or "tribe") and the Latin *cide* ("killing") to describe the systematic destruction of a group of people because of their religion, ethnicity, or other characteristics. More particularly, the 1948 United Nations Convention on the Prevention and Punishment of the Crime of Genocide (CPPCG) defined genocide as "any of the following acts committed with intent to destroy, in whole or in part, a national, ethnical, racial or religious group, as such: killing members of the group; causing serious bodily or mental harm to members of the group; deliberately inflicting on the group conditions of life calculated to bring about its physical destruction in whole or in part; imposing measures intended to prevent births within the group; [and] forcibly transferring children of the group to another group."

Ancient examples that satisfy at least some of the elements of genocide come from the Old Testament, when God requests that the Hebrews exterminate the Amalekite tribe: "Do not spare them, but kill both man and woman, and infant and nursing child, ox and sheep, camel and donkey" (1 Samuel 15:3). As for frequently cited twentieth-century examples, consider the extermination of around six million European Jews, Roma, and other groups by Nazi Germany during World War II. Also, the 1915 massacre of Armenians by the Turkish-led Ottoman Empire involved the deportation of women, children, the elderly, and infirm on death marches to the Syrian desert. In a hundred-day period in 1994, the Hutu majority massacred as many as one million Tutsis and moderate Hutus in the African state of Rwanda. As Belgian politician Alain Destexhe has noted, genocide goes beyond the meaning of mass murder, a term that does not account for the motive of genocide, which may involve killing people simply because they exist or because they are considered to be part of a worthless or hostile group—pests, like lice or fleas, to be exterminated. The instances of "ethnic cleansing" cited above, combined with increased international cooperation over the last century, led to the creation of the International Criminal Court in 2002.

See also Capital Punishment (c. 1772 BCE), Guillotine (1792), Extinction (1796), *On Death and Dying* (1969), Death Squads (1980), Thanatourism (1996)

Wat Thmey killing-field memorial (Siem Reap, Cambodia). During the 1970s, the Khmer Rouge regime executed over one million people, including those suspected of having ties with the former government or foreign governments, Cambodian Christians, Buddhist monks, and intellectuals, as well as ethnic Vietnamese, Thai, and Chinese.

KAMIKAZE PILOTS

MOTOHARU OKAMURA (1901-1948), ICHIZO HAYASHI (C. 1922-1945)

THE WORD *KAMIKAZE* (MEANING "DIVINE wind") refers to the Japanese pilots who committed suicide in World War II by intentionally crashing their planes into enemy targets, especially ships. Japanese naval aviator Motoharu Okamura proposed these attacks, which began in 1944 in a desperate response to superior U.S. military forces. The planes often were loaded with additional explosives, and at least forty-seven Allied vessels were sunk in the attacks. Roughly 4,000 kamikaze pilots lost their lives. Generally speaking, the kamikaze pilots were much less experienced and trained than Allied fighters, often making the suicide planes relatively easy targets.

Although some kamikaze pilots were motivated by patriotism and proud to die for the cause, the kamikaze training was often cruel and torturous, including severe facial beatings and coercion. Terrorism expert Ariel Merari writes, "The Kamikaze pilots demonstrate that the promise of [religious] paradise is not a necessary factor in the willingness to carry out suicide attacks. . . . The kamikaze phenomenon is a demonstration of the power of the military organization as a source of extreme social pressure."

Pilots were told never to close their eyes as they approached their targets, as they wore their special headbands and a "belt of a thousand stitches," sewn by a thousand women making one stitch each. Before kamikaze pilots embarked on their missions, they often composed and read a death poem in a tradition dating back to the samurai. One such poem read: "I memorized 300 poems at school. I was a wise boy—women winked at the market—I was all aflame with their charm. Now, I burn."

In his last letter home before his final flight in April 1945, kamikaze pilot Ichizo Hayashi wrote, "I am pleased to have the honor of having been chosen as a member of a Special Attack Force that is on its way into battle. . . . When I reflect on the hopes you had for my future . . . I feel so sad that I am going to die without doing anything to bring you joy."

See also Suicide (c. 300 BCE), Martyr (c. 135), Children and *Capacocha* (1622), Last Words of the Dying (1922)

The USS *Bunker Hill* aircraft carrier was hit by two kamikazes in May 1945, killing nearly 400 personnel.

THE GRASS HARP

TRUMAN STRECKFUS PERSONS, AKA TRUMAN CAPOTE (1924–1984)

HE GRASS HARP, A 1951 NOVEL BY AMERICAN author Truman Capote, describes a mystical method for communicating with the dead that has left readers enchanted for decades. Dolly Talbo, one of the main characters in the story, tells of hearing the voices of the departed in the sounds of windswept grass.

Early in the book, Dolly describes a field near a hillside **cemetery** with high Indian grass that changes color with the seasons. The reader imagines seeing the grass "when it has gone red as sunset, when scarlet shadows like firelight breeze over it and the autumn winds strum on its dry leaves sighing human music, a harp of voices." Soon, Dolly asks, "Do you hear? That is the grass harp, always telling a story—it knows the stories of all the people on the hill, of all the people who ever lived, and when we are dead it will tell ours, too." Dolly can even hear the voice of her dead father in the grass when the wind "gathers and remembers all our voices, then sends them talking and telling through the leaves and the fields."

Throughout the ages, many people have used the randomness of nature in attempts to communicate with spirits or divine the future. For example, the ancients sometimes interpreted cloud movements, lightning, the sounds of streams and rustling leaves, the flight of birds, the behavior of chickens when fed, and the paths of sacred horses. In modern times, listeners have attempted to discern the voices of the dead in recordings containing background noise (see **Electronic Voice Phenomena**).

In some ancient cultures, austromancers (those who base predictions on wind movements) listened to seashells held to the ear to help foretell the future. Occult scholar Donald Tyson writes, "If you listen to the seashell, and allow it to lull your mind into a receptive state, soon you will begin to make out fragments of distant conversation. . . . As this ghostly garden becomes clearer, you may find that one or more of the voices will . . . engage you in conversation."

See also: Necromancy (c. 850 BCE), Cemeteries (1831), Séance (1848), *Ophelia* (1852), "The Monkey's Paw" (1902), Electronic Voice Phenomena (1956)

Dolly hears the voices of the dead in the sounds of grasses blowing in the wind near a hillside cemetery. The grass harp "gathers and remembers all our voices, then sends them talking and telling through the leaves and the fields."

CARDIOPULMONARY RESUSCITATION

JAMES OTIS ELAM, (1918–1995), PETER SAFAR (1924–2003)

CARDIOPULMONARY RESUSCITATION (CPR) IS AN emergency technique used to maintain the life of a person who is usually in cardiac arrest and exhibiting little or no breathing. This technique often is employed until additional medical help arrives. CPR may involve chest compressions (repeatedly pushing down on the chest to encourage blood circulation), mouth-to-mouth (MM) breathing, or the use of a device to push air into the lungs. CPR also may involve use of electric shocks to encourage a normal heartbeat. Today, greater emphasis is placed on chest compressions than on artificial breathing in many emergencies, particularly when CPR is performed by untrained people.

In 1956, Austrian physician Peter Safar began human experiments to determine if MM resuscitation, in which one person blew air into another person's mouth, provided sufficient oxygen to keep the victim alive. In particular, he administered curare (a poison) to thirty-one volunteers to paralyze their breathing muscles. By monitoring levels of blood oxygen and carbon dioxide for several hours while inflating the lungs with exhaled air, he was able to demonstrate that the exhaled air had sufficient oxygen to validate the concept of MM resuscitation. On the basis of his research and the research of physicians such as James Elam, Safar encouraged a Norwegian doll maker to manufacture Resusci Anne, a mannequin for CPR training. In his 1957 book *ABC of Resuscitation,* Safar also suggested a combined approach in which a rescuer checked the airway of a victim, facilitated breathing, and performed chest compressions. The book provided a basis for worldwide training in CPR, and Safar went on to study other methods of saving lives, including therapeutic cooling, which may allow a pulseless trauma victim to survive for an additional two hours without brain damage (see **Cryonics**).

The Old Testament mentions the prophet Elisha putting his mouth upon a child and resuscitating him. In 1767, the Dutch Humane Society published guidelines suggesting that rescuers keep drowning victims warm, provide mouth-to-mouth ventilation, and blow the "smoke of burning tobacco into the rectum." Other methods evolved that were occasionally useful, including laying the victim facedown over a barrel and rolling him back and forth. Alternatively, the victim was placed facedown on a trotting horse.

See also Resurrection (c. 30 CE), Premature Burial (1844), Cryonics (1962), Brain Death (1968), Do Not Resuscitate (1976)

In the Hebrew Bible (2 Kings 4), the prophet Elisha places his mouth on the mouth of a dead boy, and the child returns to life. This depiction of Elisha and the boy was painted in 1854 by Russian artist Pavel Fedorovich Pleshanov (1829–1882).

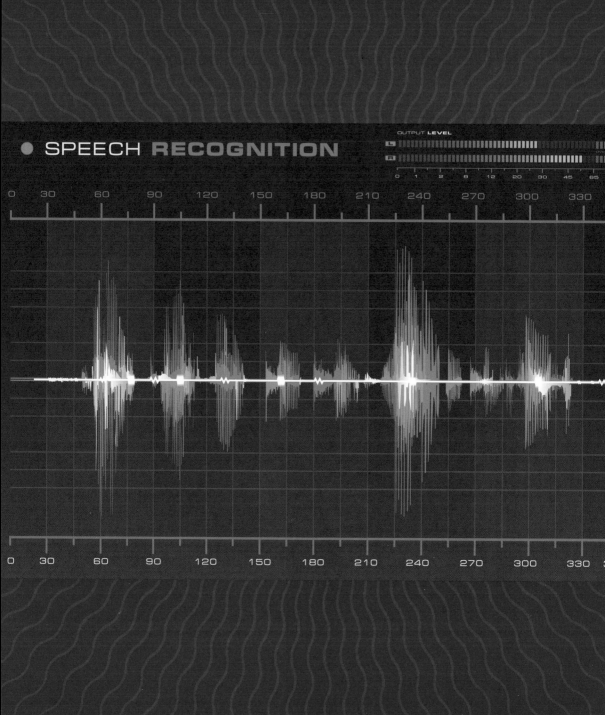

ELECTRONIC VOICE PHENOMENA

THOMAS ALVA EDISON (1847–1931), NIKOLA TESLA (1856–1943),
FRIEDRICH JÜRGENSON (1903–1987), KONSTANTĪNS RAUDIVE (1909–1974),
ERNST SENKOWSKI (B. 1922), SARAH WILSON ESTEP (1926–2008)

NIKOLA TESLA, THE SERBIAN-BORN INVENTOR and electrical engineer famous for his work with alternating current (AC) electricity, gave a speech in 1917 in which he confessed his belief that "the greatest mysteries of our being are still to be fathomed and . . . death itself may not be the termination of the wonderful metamorphoses we witness." In 1920, the American inventor Thomas Edison said in an interview, later published in *Scientific American*, that nobody knows whether "our personalities pass on to another existence or sphere" but "it is possible to construct an apparatus which will be so delicate that if there are personalities in another existence or sphere who wish to get in touch with us in this existence or sphere, this apparatus will at least give them a better opportunity to express themselves than the . . . ouija boards and mediums. . . ."

Today, electronic voice phenomena (EVP) refers to mysterious sounds that resemble speech in amplified recordings with background noise. Of course, skeptics suggest that any "voices" overheard could be the result of pareidolia, in which random stimuli are perceived to have some undue significance, such as seeing the face of the Virgin Mary in clouds.

Around 1956, American photographer Attila von Szalay believed he had recorded spirit voices by using a reel-to-reel tape recorder, although it is notable that the discarnate people had only mundane messages such as "This is G!" "Hot dog, Art!" and "Merry Christmas and Happy New Year to you all." Around 1959, Swedish painter and filmmaker Friedrich Jürgenson kindled enthusiasm in EVP when he reported hearing his dead mother calling his name during a playback of a recording he made of birds in the forest. Other famous researchers or promoters in the field include the Latvian psychologist Konstantīns Raudive, Sarah Estep (who founded the American Association of Electronic Voice Phenomena in 1982), and German professor Ernst Senkowski, who in the 1970s coined the related term *Instrumental Trans-Communication* (ITC), which encompasses the recording of communication on a range of devices, including fax machines, television screens, and digital computers.

See also Necromancy (c. 850 BCE), Séance (1848), Searches for the Soul (1907), *The Grass Harp* (1951)

EVP refers to mysterious sounds that resemble speech in amplified recordings with background noise. In the speech waveform shown here, time proceeds along the horizontal axis, and sound amplitude along the vertical axis.

I. Stromo
I. Sandoe
I. Suydro
Isles de
Fero
I. Vust
Fulo
I. de Schetland
75
I. Sand
I. Panonia
I. Faire
Isles Orcades
C. Dungusby
C. de Nos
I. Lewis
G. de Muray
I St. Kildas
Buchannes
Isles de
l'Ouest
Elgin
Aberdiene
Rokol
Edimbourg
Barvic
Carlile
Londonderi
Yorc
Galloway
Dublin
Chester
B. de Galloway
Limerik
Boston
Yarmouth
Cardigan
Oxford
Londres
les Skilings
Corke
G. de S. Georges
Weymouth
Falmouth
Douvre
C. Clare
C. Cornual
I. de Wight
MANCHE
LA
les Sorlingues
C. Lezard.
Honfleur
I. d'Ouessant
Malo
Brest

GOLDING'S LIMINAL WORLD

WILLIAM GERALD GOLDING (1911–1993), TERENCE FRANCIS EAGLETON (B. 1943)

IMAGINE THE UTTER CONFUSION OF DYING IN AN island universe perhaps millimeters away from our own in another dimension, with tendrils of consciousness uniting the past and present. The mystical image of an afterlife universe filled with strange weather and rocky shores was made famous in William Golding's 1956 novel *Pincher Martin*, in which the protagonist is the only survivor of a torpedoed destroyer during World War II. Martin is shipwrecked on a remote rocky island and tries to survive by finding small water puddles and sea plants. During the climax of the book, he encounters a storm with black lightning. British literary theorist Terry Eagleton writes that if we have failed to be giving people in life, we "will be trapped like . . . Pincher Martin in a **hell** which is the inability to die. By the end of Golding's novel, Martin has dwindled to a pair of huge, lobster-like claws tenaciously protecting his dark centre of selfhood from the 'black lightning' of God's ruthless mercy."

The reader slowly discerns that Martin has died in our real universe early in the book, giving the reader a shock by suggesting the possibility of the persistence of consciousness after death. Author Philip Redpath writes that the "black lightning is a manifestation of divine power and for God to be compassionate and merciless at the same time. . . . Golding is obscure because words fail to render for him what the truth is behind divine justice and retribution. Paradox is the closest he can get to capturing the truth." Golding describes the black lightning as probing the claws and "wearing them away in a compassion that was timeless and without mercy."

Unlike other entries in this book concerning **near-death experiences**, Plato's story of Er, or *The Epic of Gilgamesh*, Martin is unable to spread the news about the liminal world on the threshold of ordinary perception and existence. When Golding was asked to explain his mysterious ending in a radio interview, he replied, "To achieve salvation, individuality—the persona—must be destroyed. But suppose the man is nothing but greed? His original spirit . . . is hopelessly obscured by his thirst for separate individual life. What can he do at death but refuse to be destroyed [and] inhabit a world he invents from half-remembered scraps of physical life?"

See also *The Epic of Gilgamesh* (c. 2000 BCE), Hell (c. 400 BCE), Outer Darkness (c. 80 CE), *The Death of Ivan Ilyich* (1886), Afterlife in a Simulation (1967), Near-Death Experiences (1975), Quantum Immortality (1987)

Rockall (or Rokol)—a small, uninhabited remote rocky islet in the North Atlantic Ocean—has often been suggested as the mysterious afterlife setting of *Pincher Martin*. This 1772 map prepared by French geographer Jacques Nicolas Bellin (1703–1772) shows the region around Rockall.

TRANSHUMANISM

JULIAN SORELL HUXLEY (1887–1975), MAX MORE (B. 1964)

I N *NEW BOTTLES FOR NEW WINE* (1957), BIOLOGIST Julian Huxley coined the term *transhumanism* when he suggested that "the human species can . . . transcend itself—not just sporadically, an individual here in one way, an individual there in another way, but in its entirety, as humanity, [with man] transcending himself, by realizing new possibilities of and for his human nature. . . . The human species will be on the threshold of a new kind of existence, as different from ours as ours is from that of Peking man. It will at last be consciously fulfilling its real destiny."

The modern idea of transhumanism as it is espoused by the philosopher-futurist Max More and many others usually involves the use of technology to enhance human mental and physical capacities to gradually make people "posthuman." In light of our technological progress and understanding of the biological basis of aging, we may even become immortal in this century through genetic manipulation, robotics, nanotechnology, computers, or uploading minds to virtual worlds. Immortality is not such a rare thing; some invertebrates, such as certain species of hydra and jellyfish, are essentially immortal.

If your body could survive indefinitely, would "you" actually persist? All of us are changed by our experiences, and these changes are usually gradual, which means that you are nearly the same person that you were a year ago. However, if your normal or enhanced body survived continuously for a thousand years, gradual mental changes would accumulate, and perhaps an entirely different person eventually would inhabit your body. The thousand-year-old person—this orchidaceous Ozymandias—might be nothing like you. There would be no moment of death at which you had ceased to exist, but you would slowly fade away over the millennia like a sugar cube dissolving in water or like a sand castle being transformed by an ocean of time.

See also *The Epic of Gilgamesh* (c. 2000 BCE), *Frankenstein* (1818), Cryonics (1962), Afterlife in a Simulation (1967), Quantum Immortality (1987), Programmed Cell Death (2002)

American scientist and economist Yoshihiro Francis Fukuyama (b. 1952) has called transhumanism—which usually involves the use of technology to enhance human mental and physical capacities—the world's most dangerous idea.

1957

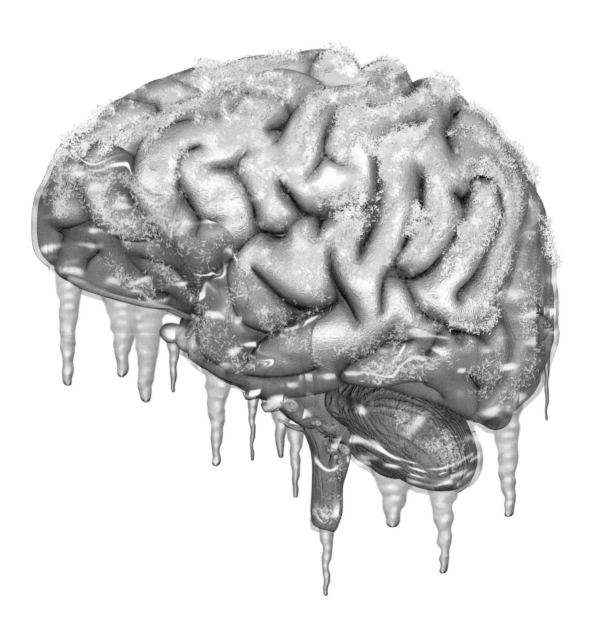

CRYONICS

BENJAMIN FRANKLIN (1709–1790), ROBERT CHESTER WILSON ETTINGER (1918–2011)

I N 1773, AMERICAN STATESMAN BENJAMIN FRANK-lin regretted that he lived "in a century too little advanced, and too near the infancy of science" so that he could not be preserved and revived to satisfy his "very ardent desire to see and observe the state of America a hundred years hence." Perhaps Franklin would have used today's cryonics facilities, in which people are preserved after they are pronounced legally dead by replacing their blood with protective fluids and cooling their bodies for long-term storage. These *cryoprotectants* reduce ice crystal formation that otherwise could damage tissues. Cryonicists hope that the technology of the future will be sufficiently advanced to revive such patients and cure whatever diseases they have. Further, if our thoughts depend primarily on the brain's structure, perhaps brains made of other materials or even simulated in software could think.

If cryonic resurrection seems far-fetched, recall that frozen embryos are routinely resurrected to produce healthy children. The modern era of cryonics was stimulated by author Robert Ettinger's book *The Prospect of Immortality*, published in 1962, which discusses the possibility of preserving human beings. Today, liquid nitrogen is used to store bodies or heads at temperatures of around –320 degrees Fahrenheit (–196 degrees Celsius). In 2006, the surgeon Hasan Alam placed pigs in a state of suspended animation; his cold pigs had no pulse, no blood, and no electrical activity in their brains, and their tissues consumed no oxygen. After a few hours, Alam pumped warm blood into the animals, and they jolted back to life. According to Alam, "Once the heart starts beating and the blood starts pumping, voila, you've got another animal that's come back from the other side. . . . Technically I think we can do it in humans."

For religious readers to ponder: If scientists were able to freeze your disembodied brain and then revive you in a century, did you enter the afterlife during the intervening time of zero brain activity?

See also Mummies (c. 5050 BCE), Autopsy (1761), *Frankenstein* (1818), Embalming (1867), Searches for the Soul (1907), Transhumanism (1957), Brain Death (1968), Near-Death Experiences (1975), Programmed Cell Death (2002)

1962

In cryonics facilities, human heads (with or without bodies) may be preserved by replacing blood with protective fluids and cooling them for long-term storage. The cryoprotectants reduce ice crystal formation, as shown in this artistic rendering, that otherwise could damage tissues.

ONDINE'S CURSE

PARACELSUS (1493–1541), JEAN GIRAUDOUX (1882–1944)

"AH, SLEEP. SWEET, BLISSFUL SLEEP," WRITES author Ian Landau. "Is there anything better than sinking into your bed when you're completely drained and drifting off to dreamland? Well, *what if you lived in fear of falling asleep*, because the simple act of slipping into unconsciousness was enough to kill you?" This is the terror of those afflicted with Ondine's curse: a medical disorder in which a patient can consciously inhale and exhale, but at night, when consciousness fades, breathing may stop. The disorder is named after Ondine (or Undine), a folkloric water nymph with an unfaithful lover who is cursed by having to remember to breathe and hence dies.

More formally referred to as congenital central hypoventilation syndrome (CCHS), Ondine's curse is a rare congenital disorder of the central nervous system, although an acquired form can develop as a result of trauma to the brainstem later in life. Mutations of the PHOX2B gene are present in many cases of CCHS, and this gene produces a protein that is involved in the development of neurons. The medical use of the term *Ondine's curse* first appeared in 1962 in a research paper describing adult patients who developed the disorder after surgery of the upper spinal cord and brainstem. Those afflicted with Ondine's curse may require tracheostomies and mechanical ventilation to survive.

Ondine also appears in the writings of Paracelsus, a Swiss-German medieval physician, who describes sprites that resemble human beings and that inhabit neighboring worlds that are largely unknown to us with our limited senses. In *Ondine*, a 1938 play by French dramatist Jean Giraudoux, knight-errant Hans falls in love with Ondine, a water sprite whom he meets in a forest near a lake.

The clinical neuroscientist and poet Raymond Tallis dramatically writes about Ondine's curse: "Our heads are endlessly trafficking with the atmosphere. From the first intaken breath, which quickly modulates into a howl, to the last gasp, there is a constant passage of air through the mouth and nose. Life and breath go together."

See also Premature Burial (1844), Cardiopulmonary Resuscitation (1956)

This photograph by Carl Van Vechten (1880–1964) shows the actress Marian Seldes (1928–2014) as Bertha in a 1954 adaptation of French playwright Jean Giraudoux's *Ondine*. In the story, Princess Bertha is part of a complex love triangle with her betrothed, Hans, and the water-sprite, Ondine.

AFTERLIFE IN A SIMULATION

KONRAD ZUSE (1910–1995), MARTIN REES (B. 1942), PAUL CHARLES WILLIAM DAVIES (B. 1946)

AS WE LEARN MORE ABOUT THE UNIVERSE AND are able to simulate complex worlds by using computers, even serious scientists are beginning to question the nature of reality. German engineer Konrad Zuse pioneered the hypothesis that the universe is a digital computer in 1967. Could we be living in a computer simulation, or could we perhaps spend our afterlives in a simulated reality once our minds are uploaded to computer chips?

In our own small pocket of the universe, we have developed computers with the ability to simulate lifelike behaviors by using software and mathematical rules. One day, we may create thinking beings that live in simulated spaces as complex and vibrant as a rain forest. Perhaps we'll be able to simulate reality itself, and it is possible that more advanced beings already are doing this elsewhere in the universe.

What if the number of these simulations is larger than the number of universes? Astronomer Martin Rees suggests that if the simulations outnumber the universes, "as they would if one universe contained many computers making many simulations," it is likely that we are artificial life. Rees writes, "Once you accept the idea of the multiverse . . .

it's a logical consequence that in some of those universes there will be the potential to simulate parts of themselves, and you may get a sort of infinite regress, so we don't know where reality stops . . . and we don't know what our place is in this grand ensemble of universes and simulated universes."

Astrophysicist Paul Davies has noted, "Eventually, entire virtual worlds will be created inside computers, their conscious inhabitants unaware that they are the simulated products of somebody else's technology. For every original world, there will be a stupendous number of available virtual worlds—some of which would even include machines simulating virtual worlds of their own, and so on ad infinitum."

If you could opt for hundreds of years of subjective time in a blissful simulated afterlife, would you do it? Perhaps you could think more clearly, love more deeply, discover new realities, be more creative, and achieve a state of fulfillment, peace, adventure, and/or accomplishment not possible in the real world.

See also Golding's Liminal World (1956), Transhumanism (1957), Quantum Immortality (1987), Quantum Resurrection (>100 Trillion)

As computers become more powerful, perhaps someday we will be able to simulate entire worlds—fanciful and realistic—and reality itself.

HOSPICE

JEANNE GARNIER (1811–1853), CICELY MARY SAUNDERS (1918–2005),
ELISABETH KÜBLER-ROSS (1926–2004)

THE TERM *HOSPICE* REFERS TO BOTH A philosophy and an approach to caring for the terminally ill, and it often involves reducing pain and addressing the psychological and spiritual needs of the dying. Such care may take place in a hospital, a nursing home, or an individual's home.

In the fourteenth century, the Knights Hospitaller of St. John of Jerusalem, a Christian military order, opened a hospicelike facility on the Greek island of Rhodes to care for the sick and dying. In 1842, the widow and bereaved mother Jeanne Garnier helped found the hospice of L'Association des Dames du Calvaire in Lyon, France

One of the most important founders of the modern hospice was British nurse, physician, and writer Cicely Saunders, who defined the mission of the hospice movement when she said, "We do not have to cure to heal." In 1967, she opened St. Christopher's Hospice in South London.

At about the same time Saunders was promoting hospice care in the United States and England, along with the notion that dying did not have to be a painful and bleak experience, the Swiss-born psychiatrist Elisabeth Kübler-Ross was studying how hospitals and society responded to terminal illness. In her 1972 testimony to the U.S. Senate Special Committee on Aging, Kübler-Ross stated, "We live in a very particular death-denying society. We isolate both the dying and the old, and it serves a purpose. They are reminders of our own mortality. We should not institutionalize people. We can give families more help with home care and visiting nurses, giving the families and the patients the spiritual, emotional, and financial help in order to facilitate the final care at home."

As for Saunders, she died at age 87 in the London hospice she founded. Before she died, she wrote, "You matter because you are you. You matter to the last moment of your life, and we will do all we can, not only to help you die peacefully, but also to live until you die."

See also *The Death of Ivan Ilyich* (1886) Cryonics (1962), *On Death and Dying* (1969), Near-Death Experiences (1975), Do Not Resuscitate (1976)

This painting by Dominique Papety (1815–1849) shows the 1291 siege of Acre (northern Israel), with the Hospitaller Master Matthieu de Clermont defending the city walls from Muslim invaders. Not long afterward, the Knights Hospitaller of St. John of Jerusalem retreated to the island of Rhodes, where they founded the first hospice.

BRAIN DEATH

"LONG BEFORE MODERN TECHNOLOGY, DEATH WAS considered to have occurred when heartbeat and breathing ceased, and the soul abandoned the body," writes the neuroscientist Calixto Machado. "Nonetheless, the concept of death evolved as technology progressed, forcing medicine and society to redefine the ancient cardiorespiratory diagnosis to a neurocentric diagnosis of death."

According to one definition, brain death is the permanent cessation of all brain function, as may occur when the blood or oxygen supply to the brain is stopped by cardiac arrest, a stroke, or a blood clot. Although the heart may still beat, the body will make no effort to breathe unaided. A brain-dead person usually is considered legally dead and can have organs harvested for donation. In 1968, Harvard Medical School published a landmark report that defined the criteria for brain death. Although electroencephalography (EEG) can be used to provide evidence of brain death, it is not infallible because the electrical activity of the brain can be so low that it is difficult to detect. To declare someone brain-dead, no brainstem reflexes should be apparent. The pupils should not react to light. The eyes should not shiver in response to ice water splashed in the ear or move when poked with a cotton swab. No gag reflex should exist. Unlike people in a persistent vegetative state (PVS), who can breathe unaided and can show signs of wakefulness such as opening their eyes, brain-dead people are considered to have no chance of recovery. Before declaring a person brain-dead, medical personnel must try to rule out conditions that may mimic aspects of brain death, such as hypothermia and overdoses of barbiturates and other drugs.

Still, the line between life and death is a murky one. The brain-dead will still have organs that function and wounds that heal. They sometimes can react to a scalpel cut the way inadequately anesthetized live patients do, exhibiting high blood pressure or a faster heart rate. They can shiver and move their arms, and they can be sexually responsive when stroked. Mothers have given birth to children after having been brain-dead for months.

See also Premature Burial (1844), Euthanasia (1872), Searches for the Soul (1907), Lovecraft's Reanimator (1922), Cardiopulmonary Resuscitation (1956), Cryonics (1962), Near-Death Experiences (1975), Do Not Resuscitate (1976), Programmed Cell Death (2002), Death of Universe (>100 Trillion)

Created for the use of a monk, this ivory pendant (c. 1600) at the Walters Art Museum in Baltimore illustrates the fuzzy line between life and death. For example, brain-dead people still have organs that function, wounds that heal, and reactions to stimuli.

ZOMBIES

ZORA NEALE HURSTON (1891-1960), GEORGE ANDREW ROMERO (B. 1940),
EDMUND WADE DAVIS (B. 1953)

ZOMBIE EXPERT NATHAN BROWN NOTES THAT death is "the great equalizer." Death "comes for us all, and none of us are exempt from its cold and final embrace. [Death] is one of the very few undeniable and absolute truths of human existence. Perhaps this is why the idea of something that could trump this great truth is so terrifying. . . . What could humanity do if death ceased to be the final destination of the living?"

Zombies usually are thought of as animated corpses that are maintained by magical or possibly scientific means. Today, their popularity in movies instills a sense of horror as they are portrayed with shambling footsteps, slack jaws, and sometimes rotting flesh. They also multiply at a frightening rate. One of the landmarks in the growth of the modern popular interest in zombies is the 1968 movie *Night of the Living Dead* directed by George A. Romero, who sometimes is nicknamed the "Godfather of Zombies."

The actual concept of zombies goes back many years. For example, according to the ideas of the Haitian Vodou religion, which stems from West African Vodun, the deceased can be reanimated by a bokor, or sorcerer. A famous early case from 1937 involves anthropologist and author Zora Neale Hurston, who reported on an alleged female zombie in Haiti. The ethnobotanist Wade Davis has made the provocative claim that the appearance of death and resurrection that is used to produce Haitian zombies might be created by using tetrodotoxin, a poisonous substance found in the puffer fish.

The contemplation of zombies forces us to confront our fears and our various attitudes to the mystery of death as well as the associated loss of control. Zombie experts Christopher Moreman and Cory Rushton write, "Zombies, as an abject reflection of our individual mortality, and harbingers of societal decay, force the viewer to consider the dark possibilities of a meaningless existence. . . . By examining the dark side that is the living dead, we might come to recognize something of ourselves as the dying alive."

See also Golem (1580), *Frankenstein* (1818), Vampires (1819), "The Monkey's Paw" (1902), Lovecraft's Reanimator (1922)

Recent popular zombie films and television shows such as *The Walking Dead* often portray zombies as humans infected with a mind-altering pathogen resulting from a disease pandemic or biological weapon.

ON DEATH AND DYING

ELISABETH KÜBLER-ROSS (1926-2004)

ONE OF THE MOST FAMOUS MODERN-DAY EXPL-orers of death was Elisabeth Kübler-Ross, the psychiatrist whose pioneering work with terminally ill patients helped revolutionize attitudes toward the care of the dying. She also spent part of her career doing research to verify the existence of life after death. After conducting thousands of interviews with people who had **near-death experiences**, she believed she had acquired sufficient evidence of an afterlife.

Her early interest in death and dying jelled when she visited World War II concentration camps. In Maidanek (also spelled Majdanek), a Polish death camp, she discovered butterflies that prisoners etched into the walls before they died:

It started in Maidanek . . . where I tried to see how children had gone into the gas chambers after having lost their families, their homes, their schools. . . . The walls in the camp were filled with pictures of butterflies, drawn by these children. It was incomprehensible to me. Thousands of children going into the gas chamber, and this is the message they leave behind—a butterfly.

In 1962, one of her lectures had a profound impact on her and her class when she invited a teenage girl who was dying of leukemia. The medical students in the audience asked about the girl's blood tests and other related medical questions. The girl told them they were insane. Why weren't they asking her questions about what it *felt* like never to dream of going to the high-school prom or even grow up? Why didn't doctors ever tell her the truth? At the end of the lecture, the students wept. Dr. Kübler-Ross nodded, telling the students that they now knew how to have compassion.

In her 1969 book *On Death and Dying*, Kübler-Ross hypothesized that dying patients often go through five stages of grief: denial, anger, bargaining, depression, and finally acceptance. She also found that most of the dying could accept death most easily if they could look back and feel that they had not wasted their lives.

See also Death's-Head Hawk Moth (1846), Walking Corpse Syndrome (1880), *The Death of Ivan Ilyich* (1886), Last Words of the Dying (1922), Genocide (1944), Hospice (1967), Near-Death Experiences (1975)

1969

In this memento mori painting, French painter Philippe de Champaigne (1602–1674) conveys the brevity of life and the inevitability of death with a flower, a skull, and an hourglass.

NEAR-DEATH EXPERIENCES

PLATO (428–348 BCE), HIERONYMUS BOSCH (1450–1516),
RABINDRANATH TAGORE (1861–1941), RAYMOND MOODY (B. 1944)

THE BENGALI POET RABINDRANATH TAGORE wrote, "Death is not extinguishing the light; it is putting out the lamp because the dawn has come." Scientists and mystics have long pondered the physical and mental transitions that occur at the threshold of death. In 1975, physician Raymond Moody published his bestselling book *Life After Life*, which provided cases studies of people who were without vital signs (and some who were pronounced dead by their physicians) and later revived. Some of the people had NDEs, or *near-death experiences* (a term Moody coined), in which they felt that they were leaving their bodies and floating up to the ceiling. During an NDE, others saw a light at the end of a tunnel and felt serenity or a subsequent loss of fear of death, although a smaller percentage experienced heightened distress. Some reported seeing the doctors performing medical resuscitation efforts.

Although some researchers have suggested that NDEs provide evidence of life after death or perhaps a movement of consciousness away from the body, others explain such phenomena in purely biological terms, suggesting that the experiences are hallucinations caused by a brain deprived of oxygen (hypoxia) or excess carbon dioxide in the blood (hypercarbia). Some have theorized that brain chemicals called endorphins may create the euphoric sensations of NDEs. Researchers have experimented with the hallucinogen ketamine, which can produce an altered state of consciousness resembling an NDE. However, even if the NDEs are hallucinations, physicians study them to better understand their mechanism and because they often have a profound, lasting psychological effect on the person who has the experience.

Of course, the idea of NDEs is not new. In *The Republic,* Plato tells the story of Er, a soldier who is killed and journeys toward "a straight light like a pillar, most nearly resembling a rainbow, but brighter and purer." Er later returns to life to spread the news about another world. Around 1500, Dutch artist Hieronymus Bosch produced the startling painting *Ascent of the Blessed*, showing souls passing through a tunnel toward a light.

See also Searches for the Soul (1907), Cryonics (1962), Hospice (1967), Brain Death (1968), *On Death and Dying* (1969)

Ascent of the Blessed by Dutch artist Hieronymus Bosch is one of four panels (a polyptych) collectively titled *Visions of the Hereafter.*

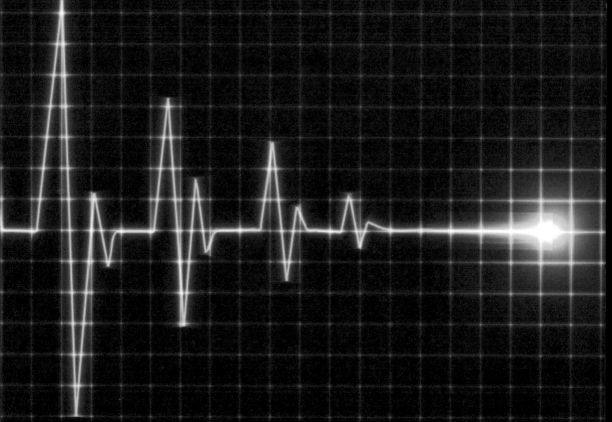

DO NOT RESUSCITATE

KAREN ANN QUINLAN (1954–1985)

CIVIL RIGHTS LEADER MARTIN LUTHER KING JR. once said, "The quality, not the longevity, of one's life is what is important." Indeed, through the most recent few decades, there have been profound debates regarding when a physician should let a terminally ill or comatose patient die. Law professor William A. Woodruff writes, "As medical technology progressed to the point where a patient's vital signs could be sustained almost indefinitely, society began to question the value of these advancements. If the patient was permanently comatose, unable to interact with his environment . . . and unable to function at even a basic cognitive level, what purpose was served in keeping him alive?"

This kind of question led to the establishment of modern do not resuscitate (DNR) orders in the United States and other countries. These legal documents allow patients or other designees to specify that resuscitation should not be attempted when a person experiences cardiac or respiratory arrest. One important step in the legalization of DNRs in the United States was the 1976 case in which the New Jersey Supreme Court upheld the right of the father of comatose Karen Ann Quinlan to have her removed from artificial ventilation. In 1991, the U.S. Patient Self-Determination Act forced hospitals to honor patients' decisions about their health care, and competent patients had the right to refuse treatment. Thus, if a DNR order is present, advanced cardiac life support will not be used and **cardiopulmonary resuscitation** will not be attempted.

Of course, DNRs introduce a certain complexity into the healthcare system. For example, with the advent of DNRs, if a patient is resuscitated in a hospital against the patient's wishes, a "wrongful life" lawsuit can be filed. Also, in the case *Payne v. Marion General Hospital* (1990), a court ruled against a physician who issued a DNR order at the request of a patient's relatives. The court found that the patient was competent a few minutes before his death and should have been consulted.

See also Euthanasia (1872), Cardiopulmonary Resuscitation (1956), Hospice (1967), Brain Death (1968), Near-Death Experiences (1975)

This artistic conception of a cardiogram shows a flat-lining pulse, indicating cardiac arrest.

DEATH SQUADS

ÓSCAR ARNULFO ROMERO Y GALDÁMEZ (1917–1980)

URING A VIOLENT CIVIL WAR THAT STARTED around 1980, the small Central American country of El Salvador became a symbol of political terror, human rights abuse, and death squads, which are known in Spanish by the name *escuadrónes de la muerte*, or "squadrons of death." In March 1980, Salvadoran Archbishop Óscar Romero was assassinated while saying Mass in a hospital chapel. The death squad responsible was found to have included soldiers in the Salvadoran military security forces. Romero was a champion of the poor who called for Salvadoran death squads to stop carrying out government repression. According to Latin America expert Cynthia J. Arnson, in November of the same year, "the entire leadership of the leftist political opposition was kidnapped from a press conference and murdered, their mutilated bodies strewn about the outskirts of the capital." In December, four U.S. missionaries were gang-raped and murdered by a military unit. Their bodies were left in a shallow grave. Arnson writes, "Over the next decade, tens of thousands of . . . Salvadorans— university professors, trade unionists . . . and humanitarian workers—lost their lives in acts of targeted or indiscriminate terror."

Death squads are not limited to Latin America but have operated all over the world, often with government support—usually in military dictatorships or police states but sometimes in democracies, especially if a state of emergency has been declared. Around 1850, during the California Gold Rush, the state government financed and organized death squads to seek out and massacre Native Americans. A large portion of the financing came from the federal government.

Although death squads have much in common with terrorists and vigilantes, some terrorists can use a somewhat random, unpredictable approach to "send a message," whereas death squads tend to focus on specific targets. Unlike death squads, vigilantes often are motivated by private and spontaneous concerns. The term *death squad* usually is not applied to soldiers fighting soldiers in wars between sovereign states.

See also Capital Punishment (c. 1772 BCE), Guillotine (1792), Genocide (1944)

During the reign of Ivan the Terrible (1530–1584), his Oprichniki suppressed perceived internal enemies through torture and murder. In *The Oprichniki*, Russian artist Nikolai Nevrev (1830–1904) depicts the final minutes of a man arrested for treason and forced to sit on a throne to mock his alleged ambitions.

QUANTUM IMMORTALITY

HANS MORAVEC (B. 1948), MAX TEGMARK (B. 1967)

THE MIND-BOGGLING IDEA OF QUANTUM immortality and related concepts discussed by technologist Hans Moravec in 1987—and later by physicist Max Tegmark—relies on the many-worlds interpretation (MWI) of quantum mechanics. This theory holds that whenever the universe ("world") is confronted by a choice of paths at the quantum level, it follows the various possibilities, splitting into multiple universes.

According to proponents of quantum immortality, the MWI implies that we may be able to live virtually forever. For example, suppose you are about to be executed in an electric chair. In almost all parallel universes, the **electric chair** will kill you. However, there is a small set of alternative universes in which you somehow survive; for example, an electrical component may fail when the executioner pulls the switch. You are alive in, and thus able to experience, one of the universes in which the electric chair malfunctions and hence live virtually forever.

Consider a thought experiment. Imagine that Bob has a brain electrode that is triggered or not triggered in accordance with the decay of a radioactive atom. With each run of the experiment, there is a 50–50 chance that the electrode will activate, painlessly killing Bob. If the MWI is correct, perhaps each time Bob conducts the experiment, he will be split into one universe in which the electrode fires and kills him and another universe in which the electrode does not fire. Perform the experiment a thousand times and Bob may find himself to be surprisingly alive. In the universe in which the electrode fires, he is dead. However, from the point of view of the living version of Bob, the electrode experiment will continue running, and he will be alive forever, because at each branch in the multiverse there will be a version of him that survives.

See also Electric Chair (1890), Transhumanism (1957), Afterlife in a Simulation (1967), Quantum Resurrection (>100 Trillion)

According to proponents of quantum immortality, we can avoid the lurking specter of death virtually forever.

THANATOURISM

1996

WHY DO PEOPLE FLOCK TO VENUES SUCH AS the London Dungeon, a tourist attraction that re-creates various gory and death-laden historical events? Related forms of thanatourism (also known as dark tourism) can serve not only as entertainment but also as a remembrance or education that involves traveling to locations associated with suffering or death, such as actual sites of assassinations or mass killings, including Ground Zero in New York City.

Stephanie Yuill, a dark-tourism expert, enumerates some of the more famous locations: "Today, numerous sites of death and disaster attract millions of visitors from all around the world: Auschwitz-Birkenau, Anne Frank's House, Graceland, Oklahoma City, Gettysburg, Vimy Ridge, the Somme, and Arlington National Cemetery." The term dark tourism became popular after several researchers applied labels to this phenomenon, including travel experts J. John Lennon and Malcolm Foley. The concept of black spots (which includes the commercialization of grave sites) was first mentioned in 1993, and British tourism professor Tony Seaton coined the term *thanatourism* in 1996.

Interest in calamity is nothing new, as evidenced by the popularity of public executions and tours of morgues in Victorian England. Lennon reminds us, "The Battle of Waterloo in 1815 was observed by nobility from a safe distance, and one of the earliest battlefields of the American Civil War (Manassas) was sold the next day as a visitor attraction site."

"How dark does real-world dark tourism get?" asks *New Scientist*. "Consider the James Dean fanatics who 're-enact' the actor's death each year at the place and time it happened, often driving cars similar to his, to experience his final moments for themselves. What they are seeking is anyone's guess." Lennon reminds us that black locations are important "testaments to the consistent failure of humanity to temper our worst excesses." If these sites are managed properly, we can "learn from the darkest elements of our past. But we have to guard against the voyeuristic and exploitative streak that is evident at so many of them."

See also Ossuaries (c. 1000 BCE), Thanatos (c. 700 BCE), Cemeteries (1831), Crucifixion Vision of Tissot (c. 1890), Genocide (1944)

The **London Dungeon** (opened in 1974) re-creates various gory and death-laden historical events. This statue appears on the museum's exterior.

PROGRAMMED CELL DEATH

2002

E WOULD NOT BE ALIVE TODAY IF IT WERE not for programmed cell death (PCD, also known as apoptosis), a regulated dying process in which cells in our bodies commit **suicide**. In fact, our fingers would contain webbing between them if this kind of cell suicide did not occur between finger regions during embryological development. The process is so important that scientists have poetically referred to PCD as "the siren's song—the death that makes life live." Molecular biologists Gerry Melino and David Vaux write, "If we imagine an 80-year-old person in which mitosis [cell division] proceeded unopposed by any balancing homeostatic death process, he would have around two square km [494 acres] of skin, two tons of bone marrow and lymph nodes, and a gut 16 km [9.9 miles] long. Indeed, mitosis unchecked by cell death results in neoplastic pathology [tumor growth]."

Published papers on PCD in insect tissue (1964) and rat liver tissue (1965) increased interest in the field. In 2002, the Nobel Prize in Physiology or Medicine was awarded to researchers who identified the genes that control apoptosis. Approximately 60 billion cells die each day in an adult human as a result of apoptosis, but too much apoptosis may be associated with diseases such as Alzheimer's and Parkinson's. Cell suicide may be triggered when cells become old and defective and self-destruct because of internal cellular programming that regulates gene and protein expression. Neighboring cells can also send chemical signals that trigger a cell to commit suicide.

Journalist Molly Edmonds writes, "When a cell is compelled to commit suicide . . . proteins called caspases go into action. They break down the cellular components needed for survival, and they spur production of enzymes known as DNases, which destroy the DNA in the nucleus of the cell. It's like roadies breaking down the stage in an arena after a major band has been through town." Macrophages, cells that act a little like vacuum cleaners, remove the dead cells.

See also Transhumanism (1957), Cryonics (1962), Brain Death (1968)

An artistic representation of apoptosis. If cells are no longer needed in a multicellular organism, these cells may commit suicide by activating an intracellular death program. Inappropriate apoptosis (either too little or too much) plays a role in autoimmune disorders, neurodegenerative diseases, and many types of cancer.

DEATH OF UNIVERSE

STEPHEN WILLIAM HAWKING (B. 1942), FRED ADAMS (B. 1961)

HE POET ROBERT FROST WROTE, "SOME SAY THE world will end in fire, some say in ice." The ultimate destiny of our universe depends on its geometrical shape, the behavior of dark energy, the amount of matter, and other factors. The astrophysicists Fred Adams and Gregory Laughlin have described the dark ending as our current star-filled cosmos eventually evolves to a vast sea of subatomic particles while stars, galaxies, and even black holes fade.

In one scenario, the death of the universe unfolds in several acts. In our *current era*, the energy generated by stars drives astrophysical processes. Even though our universe is about 13.7 billion years old, the vast majority of stars have barely begun to shine. Alas, all stars will die after 100 trillion years, and star formation will be halted because galaxies will have run out of gas, the raw material for making new stars. At this point, the stelliferous, or star-filled, era draws to a close.

During the *second era*, the universe continues to expand while energy reserves and galaxies shrink. Material clusters at galactic centers and brown dwarfs—objects that don't have sufficient mass to shine as stars do—linger on. By this point in time, gravity will have drawn together the burned-out remains of dead stars, and these shrunken objects will have formed superdense objects such as white dwarfs, neutron stars, and black holes. Eventually even the white dwarfs and neutron stars will disintegrate as a result of the decay of protons.

The *third era*—the era of black holes—is one in which gravity has turned entire galaxies into invisible, supermassive black holes. Through a process of energy radiation described by astrophysicist Stephen Hawking in the 1970s, black holes eventually may dissipate their tremendous mass. This means a black hole with the mass of a large galaxy will evaporate completely in 10^{98} to 10^{100} years.

What is left as the curtain closes on the black hole era? What fills the lonely cosmic void? Could any creatures survive? In the end, our universe may largely consist of a diffuse sea of electrons.

See also Extinction (1796), Euthanasia (1872), Quantum Resurrection (>100 Trillion)

∨100 trillion

An artistic depiction of a dying universe by Margaret M. Stewart. Astrophysicists have described the dark ending in which our current star-filled cosmos evolves to a vast sea of subatomic particles while stars, galaxies, and even black holes fade.

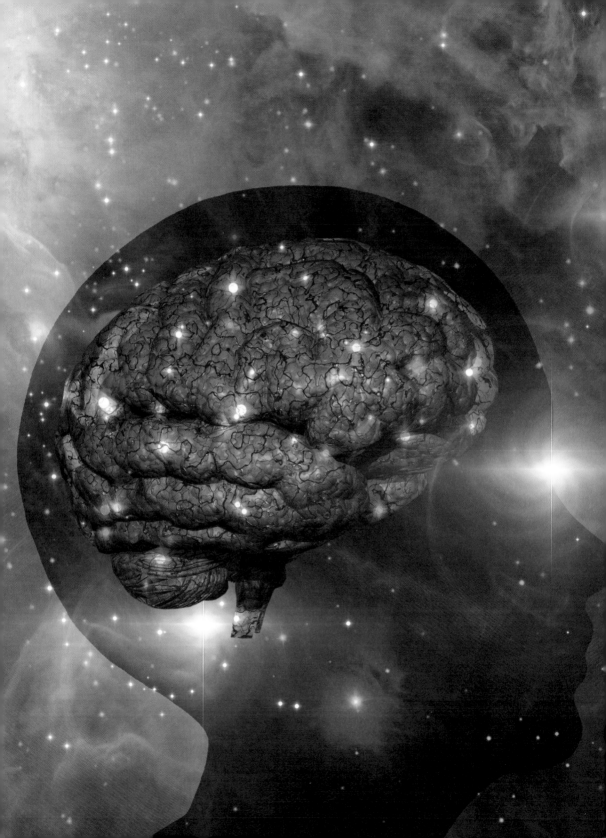

QUANTUM RESURRECTION

LUDWIG EDUARD BOLTZMANN (1844–1906), LEONARD SUSSKIND (B. 1940),
TOM BANKS (B. 1949), KATHERINE FREESE (B. 1957)

THE FATE OF OUR UNIVERSE IS UNKNOWN, AND some theories posit the continual creation of universes that "bud" from ours. However, let's focus on our own universe. One possibility is that our universe will continue to expand forever, and particles will become increasingly sparse. This seems like a sad end, doesn't it? However, even in this empty universe, quantum mechanics tells us that residual energy fields will have random fluctuations. Particles will spring out of the vacuum as if out of nowhere. Usually, this activity is small, and large fluctuations are rare. But particles do emerge, and over a long period of time something big is bound to appear (for example, a hydrogen atom or even a small molecule such as ethylene, $H_2C=CH_2$). This may seem unimpressive, but if our future is infinite, almost anything could pop into existence. Most of the gunk that emerges will be an amorphous mess, but every now and then, perhaps a tiny number of ants, planets, people, or Jupiter-size brains made from gold will emerge. Given an *infinite* amount of time, *you* will reappear, according to the physicist Katherine Freese. Quantum **resurrection** may await all of us.

Today, serious researchers even discuss the possibility of the universe being overrun by *Boltzmann* brains: self-aware, free-floating brains in outer space. Of course, the Boltzmann brains—which take their name from the Austrian physicist Ludwig Boltzmann—are highly improbable objects, and there is virtually no chance that one has appeared in the 13.7 billion years our universe has existed. According to a calculation by physicist Tom Banks, the probability of thermal fluctuations producing a brain is e to the power of -10^{25}. However, in an infinitely large space existing for an infinitely long time, these spooky conscious observers might spring into existence. Today, there is a growing literature on the implications of Boltzmann brains, kick-started by a 2002 publication by the researchers Lisa Dyson, Matthew Kleban, and Leonard Susskind that seemed to imply that the *typical* intelligent observer could possibly arise through thermal fluctuations rather than cosmology and evolution.

See also Reincarnation (c. 600 BCE), Resurrection (c. 30 CE), Afterlife in a Simulation (1967), Quantum Immortality (1987)

>100 trillion

An artistic representation of a disembodied brain in space by Bruce Rolff. Could thermally produced discarnate intelligences someday dominate our universe?

NOTES AND REFERENCES

OR FURTHER INFORMATION, IMAGES, AND context on several of the science and/ or medical entries in this book, such as quantum resurrection, cryonics, and autopsy, please see several of my previous illustrated, chronologically organized books: *The Physics Book: From the Big Bang to Quantum Resurrection* (Sterling, 2011), *The Medical Book: From Witch Doctors to Robot Surgeons* (Sterling, 2012), and *The Book of Black* (Dover, 2013).

I've compiled the following reference list that identifies some of the material I used to research and write this book. As many readers are aware, Internet websites come and go. Sometimes they change addresses or completely disappear. The website addresses listed here provided valuable background information when this book was written. Online sources such as Wikipedia (*en.wikipedia.org*) are a valuable starting point for any quest such as this one, and I sometimes used this site as a launchpad, along with many other websites, books, and research papers.

If I have overlooked an interesting or pivotal moment associated with the science and sociology of death and the afterlife that you feel has never been fully appreciated, please let me know about it. Just visit my website, *pickover.com*, and send me an e-mail explaining the idea and how you feel it influenced the world. Perhaps future editions of the book will include entries on such topics as lethal injection, crucifixion, lynching, Ouija boards, Plato's myth of Er, and Bridey Murphy, for example.

Finally, I thank Teja Krašek, Dennis Gordon, Susan Stone, and Letitia Potorac for their comments and suggestions.

Introduction

Christina, G., "Comforting Thoughts about Death that Have Nothing to Do with God," *Skeptical Inquirer*, March/April 2005, p. 50.

Kosslyn, S., chapter in *What We Believe but Cannot Prove*, ed. J. Brockman (New York: Harper, 2006).

Pickover, C., *A Beginner's Guide to Immortality* (New York: Thunder's Mouth Press, 2007).

c. 11,000 BCE: Natufian Funeral Flowers

Barras, C., "Flowers Have Been at Funerals for 13,000 Years," *New Scientist*, July 2, 2013, tinyurl.com/oqlbgvn.

Nadel, D., et al. "Earliest Floral Grave Lining from 13,700–11,700-y-old Natufian Burials at Raqefet Cave, Mt. Carmel, Israel," Proceedings of the National Academy of Sciences of the United States of America, July 16, 2013, tinyurl.com/lo5r5ux.

c. 4000 BCE: Burial Mounds

"Jefferson's Excavation of an Indian Burial Mound," *The Jefferson Monticello*, November 2010, tinyurl.com/c6owtx2.

Orchard, A., *A Critical Companion to Beowulf* (Suffolk, UK: D. S. Brewer, 2003).

c. 4000 BCE: Coffins

De Witte, M., *Long Live the Dead* (Amsterdam: Aksant, 2001).

c. 2400 BCE: Heaven

Lotz, A., *Heaven* (Nashville: Thomas Nelson, 2005).

Smith, G., *Heaven in the American Imagination* (New York: Oxford University Press, 2011).

c. 2000 BCE: *The Epic of Gilgamesh*

Mitchell, S., *Gilgamesh* (New York: Atria, 2004).

Sandars, N., *The Epic of Gilgamesh* (New York: Penguin Books, 1972).

c. 1772 BCE: Capital Punishment

Marzilli, A., *Capital Punishment* (New York: Chelsea House, 2008).

c. 1600 BCE: Gravestones

Greenfield, R., "Our First Parks: The Forgotten History of Cemeteries" (interview with K. Eggener), *The Atlantic*, March 16, 2011, tinyurl.com/d95o8gq.

"Stela," *Encyclopaedia Britannica*, accessed April 20, 2015, tinyurl.com/lptagh2.

c. 1550 BCE: *The Egyptian Book of the Dead*

Allsop, L., "Ancient Egyptians' Spells Were 'Passport' into Paradise," CNN.com, November 4, 2010, tinyurl.com/ms3jmm4.

Lichtheim, M., *Ancient Egyptian Literature, Vol. II* (Berkeley: University of California Press, 2006).

c. 1007 BCE: The Witch of Endor

Day, C., *The Witches' Book of the Dead* (San Francisco: Weiser, 2011).

Wray, T., *Good Girls, Bad Girls* (Lanham, MD: Rowman & Littlefield, 2008).

c. 600 BCE: Reincarnation

Dowdey, S., "How Reincarnation Works," HowStuffWorks.com, accessed April 20, 2015, tinyurl.com/n7sfjjy.

480 BCE: Epitaphs

Miller, K., *Last Laughs* (New York: Sterling, 2006).

Wright, G., *Discovering Epitaphs* (Oxford, UK: Shire, 2008).

c. 400 BCE: Hell

Crisafulli, C., and K. Thompson, *Go to Hell* (New York: Simon & Schuster, 2005).

c. 300 BCE: Suicide

Watt, J., *From Sin to Insanity* (Ithaca, NY: Cornell University Press, 2004).

c. 210 BCE: Terra-Cotta Army

Capek, M., *Emperor Qin's Terra Cotta Army* (Minneapolis, MN: Twenty-First Century Books, 2008).

c. 100 BCE: Xibalba

Chládek, S., *Exploring Maya Ritual Caves* (Lanham, MD: AltaMira, 2011).

c. 30 CE: Resurrection

Vermes, G., *The Resurrection* (New York: Doubleday, 2008).

c. 70 CE: Abortion

Guenin, L., "Morals and Primordials," *Science* 292 (June 2001):1659.

Pickover, C., *The Medical Book* (New York: Sterling, 2012).

c. 80 CE: Outer Darkness

Faust, J. D., *The Rod: Will God Spare It?* (Hayesville, NC: Schoettle Publishing Co., 2003).

Lockyer, H., *All the Parables of the Bible* (Grand Rapids, MI: Zondervan, 1988).

Pickover, C., *The Book of Black* (New York: Dover, 2013).

Williams, D., *Complete Idiot's Guide to Understanding Mormonism* (Indianapolis: Alpha, 2003).

c. 100 CE: Ghosts

Danelek, J., *The Case for Ghosts* (Woodbury, MN: Llewellyn, 2006).

c. 135: Martyr

Roth, C., *Encyclopedia Judaica* (18-volume set) (New York: Coronet Books, reprint edition, 2002).

c. 780: *The Tibetan Book of the Dead*

Bower, M. and J. Waxman, *Lecture Notes: Oncology* (Hoboken, NJ: Wiley-Blackwell, 2010).

c. 1220: Bifrost

Lee, R., and A. Fraser, *The Rainbow Bridge* (University Park, PA: Pennsylvania State University Press, 2001).

1321: Dante's *The Divine Comedy*

Kirkpatrick, R., ed., *Dante* (New York: Cambridge University Press, 2006).

SparkNotes Editors, "SparkNote on Inferno," SparkNotes, accessed April 20, 2015, tinyurl.com/cp5s5p.

1328: Sky Burial

Faison, S., "Lirong Journal: Tibetans, and Vultures, Keep Ancient Burial Rite," *New York Times*, July 3, 1999, tinyurl.com/mtys8ma.

1347: Black Death

Cantor, N., *In the Wake of the Plague: The Black Death and the World It Made* (New York: Free Press, 2001).

Marriott, E., *Plague* (New York: Metropolitan Books, 2002).

1350: Banshee

Yeats, W., *The Celtic Twilight* (London, A. H. Bullen, 1893).

1424: Grim Reaper

Aiken, L., *Dying, Death, and Bereavement* (Mahwah, NJ: Lawrence Erlbaum Associates, 2001).

c. 1490: *Death and the Miser*

Bosing, W., *The Complete Paintings of Bosch* (Los Angeles: Taschen, 2000).

Pankofsky, E., *Early Netherlandish Painting* (New York: HarperCollins, 1971).

1519: Day of the Dead

Paz, O., *The Labyrinth of Solitude* (New York; Grove Press, 1994).

Williams, K., and S. Mack, *Day of the Dead* (Layton, UT: Gibbs Smith, 2011).

c. 1590: Funeral Processions

Benjamin, K., *Funerals to Die For* (Avon, MA: Adams, 2013).

Hoy, W., *Do Funerals Matter?* (New York: Routledge, 2013).

1619: Plague Doctor Costume

Rosenhek, J., "Doctors of the Black Death," *Doctor's Review*, October 2011, tinyurl.com/kaa3swh.

1651: Gravediggers

Quigley, C., *The Corpse* (Jefferson, NC: McFarland, 1996).

Parets, M., *A Journal of the Plague Year* (Amelang, J., translator) (New York: Oxford University Press, 1991).

1731: Obituaries

Bowman, D., quoted in N. Starck, *Life After Death* (Melbourne University Publishing, 2006).

Hume, J., *Obituaries in American Culture* (Jackson: University Press of Mississippi, 2000).

Pickover, C., *A Beginner's Guide to Immortality* (New York: Thunder's Mouth Press, 2007).

1770: Death Certificate

Wexelman, B., quoted in L. Altman, "Making the Right Call, Even in Death," *New York Times*, July 1, 2013, tinyurl.com/lvfa5mg.

1792: Guillotine

Abbott, G., *What a Way to Go* (New York: St. Martin's, 2007).

c. 1805: Jacob's Ladder

Ryken, L, J. Wilhoit, and T. Longman, eds., *Dictionary of Biblical Imagery* (Downers Grove, IL: InterVarsity Press, 1998).

1818: *Frankenstein*

Goldman, M., "Origins of the Modern Prometheus," *Science*, 341 (July 2013): 131, tinyurl.com/n9mde25.

1819: Vampires

Johnson, E. M., "A Natural History of Vampires," *Scientific American* (blog), October 31, 2011, tinyurl.com/73mgtqp.

Maberry, J., *Vampire Universe* (New York: Citadel, 2006).

1831: Cemeteries

Greenfield, R., "Our First Parks: The Forgotten History of Cemeteries" (interview with K. Eggener), *The Atlantic*, March 16, 2011, tinyurl.com/d95o8gq.

1845: "The Raven"

Kennedy, J., ed, *The Portable Edgar Allan Poe* (New York: Penguin, 2006).

1845: Summer Land

Davis, A., *The Great Harmonia* (New York: B. Marsh, 1852).

Davis, A., *A Stellar Key to the Summer Land* (Los Angeles: Austin Publishing, 1920).

1846: Death's-Head Hawk Moth

Majerus, M., *Moths* (New York: Collins, 2010).

Murgoci, A., "The Vampire in Roumania," *Folk-Lore*, 37 (December, 1926).

1848: Séance

Pickover, C., *Dreaming the Future* (Amherst, NY: Prometheus, 2001).

1852: *Ophelia*

Brown, R., *The Art of Suicide* (London: Reaktion Books, 2001).

Thomas, J., "Ophelia," in *Encyclopedia of the Romantic Era, 1760–1850*, ed. C. Murray, (New York: Routledge, 2003).

1867: Embalming

Laderman, G., *Rest in Peace* (New York: Oxford University Press, 2005).

1872: Euthanasia

Dworkin, R., *Life's Dominion* (New York: Vintage, 1994).

1880: Walking Corpse Syndrome

Enoch, E., and H. Ball, *Uncommon Psychiatric Disorders*. (London: Hodder Arnold, 2001). (Source of quotes from patients.)

1886: *The Death of Ivan Ilyich*

Blythe, R., introduction to Leo Tolstoy's *The Death of Ivan Ilyich* (New York: Bantam, 1981).

c. 1888: Death Mask

Kolbe, G., foreword in *Undying Faces*, trans. M. Green (Whitefish, MT: Kennsinger, 2010). (A translation of E. Benkard's *Das Ewige Antlitz*.)

Quigley, C., *The Corpse* (Jefferson, NC: McFarland, 1996).

c. 1890: Crucifixion Vision of Tissot

Brooklyn Museum, "James Tissot: 'The Life of Christ,'" accessed April 20, 2015, tinyurl.com/lbhd2g8.

Matyjaszkiewicz, K., *James Tissot* (New York: Abbeville, 1985).

1895: Schwabe's *The Death of the Gravedigger*

Guthke, K., *The Gender of Death* (New York: Cambridge University Press, 1999).

1896: *The Garden of Death*

Bertman, S., "The Garden of Death," LITMED (Literature, Arts, Medicine Database), last modified May 17, 2007, tinyurl.com/kl962p5.

1902: "The Monkey's Paw"

Rescher, N., *Philosophical Explorations* (Piscataway, NJ: Transaction Books, 2011).

1907: Searches for the Soul

Pickover, C., *The Medical Book* (New York: Sterling, 2012).

1922: Last Words of the Dying

Bisbort, A., *Famous Last Words* (Rohnert Park, CA: Pomegranate, 2001).

Brotman, B., "Striking Similarity of Dying Words," *Chicago Tribune*, June 19, 2013, tinyurl.com/o4a4hq3.

Callanan, M., Kelley, P., *Final Gifts* (New York: Simon & Schuster, 2012).

1922: Lovecraft's Reanimator

Brite, P., introduction to *Waking Up Screaming* (New York: Del Rey, 2003).

Hambly, B., introduction to *The Road to Madness* (New York: Del Rey, 1996).

1944: Genocide

Destexhe, A., *Rwanda and Genocide in the Twentieth Century* (New York: New York University Press, 1995).

1944: Kamikaze Pilots

Merari, A., *Driven to Death* (New York: Oxford University Press, 2010).

Stevenson, J. "An Excerpt from Kamikaze Death Poetry," *SPECS Journal of Art and Culture*, 2(2009): 172.

1951: *The Grass Harp*

Tyson, D., *Scrying for Beginners* (Woodbury, MN: Llewellyn, 1997).

1956: Cardiopulmonary Resuscitation

Pickover, C., *The Medical Book* (New York: Sterling, 2012).

1956: Golding's Liminal World

Eagleton, T., *Figures of Dissent* (New York: Verso, 2003).

Golding, W., *Pincher Martin: The Two Deaths of Christopher Martin* (New York: Harvest Books, 2002).

Pickover, C., *The Book of Black* (New York: Dover, 2013).

Redpath, P., *William Golding: A Structural Reading of His Fiction* (Totowa, NJ: Barnes & Noble Books, 1986).

Surette, L., "A Matter of Belief: Pincher Martin's Afterlife," *Twentieth Century Literature*, 40 (Summer 1994): 205–225. (Source of Golding's radio quotation.)

1957: Transhumanism

Huxley, J., *New Bottles for New Wine* (London: Chatto & Windus, 1957).

Pickover, C., *A Beginner's Guide to Immortality* (New York: Thunder's Mouth Press, 2007).

1962: Cryonics

Alam, H., quoted in A. "Suspended Animation: Putting Life on Hold," *New Scientist*, January 21, 2006, tinyurl .com/4h3kku2.

Pickover, C., *The Medical Book* (New York: Sterling, 2012).

1962: Ondine's Curse

Landau, I., *The Hypochondriac's Handbook* (New York: Skyhorse Publishing, 2010).

Tallis, R., *The Kingdom of Infinite Space* (New Haven, CT: Yale University Press, 2008).

1967: Afterlife in a Simulation

Davies, P., "A Brief History of the Universe," *New York Times*, April 12, 2003, tinyurl.com/yfyap9t.

Pickover, C., *The Physics Book* (New York: Sterling, 2011).

Reese, M., "In the Matrix," Edge .org, accessed April 20, 2015, tinyurl.com/yke5b7w.

1967: Hospice

Pickover, C., *The Medical Book* (New York: Sterling, 2012).

1968: Brain Death

Machado, C., *Brain Death*: A Reappraisal (New York: Springer, 2007).

1968: Zombies

Brown, N., *The Complete Idiot's Guide to Zombies* (Indianapolis: Alpha, 2010).

Moreman, C., and C. Rushton, *Zombies Are Us* (Jefferson, NC: McFarland, 2011).

1969: *On Death and Dying*

Of course, not all patients follow all of the stages of dying, and some have criticized the idea of five stages as not being sufficiently accurate. Nevertheless, *On Death and Dying* has had a large effect on both laypeople and medical professionals.

Pickover, C., *A Beginner's Guide to Immortality* (New York: Thunder's Mouth Press, 2007).

Redwood, D., "Elisabeth Kübler-Ross, Interview" tinyurl.com /m84bsmp.

1975: Near-Death Experiences

Pickover, C., *The Medical Book* (New York: Sterling, 2012).

1976: Do Not Resuscitate

Pickover, C., *The Medical Book* (New York: Sterling, 2012).

Woodruff, W., tinyurl.com /pte2p4b.

1980: Death Squads

Arnson, C., "Window on the Past: A Declassified History of Death Squads in El Salvador." In *Death Squads in Global Perspective*, Campbell, B., and A. Brenner, eds. (New York: Palgrave, 2002).

1987: Quantum Immortality

Pickover, C., *The Physics Book* (New York: Sterling, 2011).

1996: Thanatourism

Foley, M., and J. Lennon, "JKF and Dark Tourism: A Fascination with Assassination," *International Journal of Heritage Studies 2* (1996): 198–211.

Foley, M., and J. Lennon, "Dark Tourism: An Ethical Dilemma," in *Strategic Issues for the Hospitality: Tourism and Leisure Industries*, eds. M. Foley, J. J. Lennon, and G. Maxwell (London: Cassell, 1997), pp. 153–164.

Lennon, J., "Journeys into Understanding: What Is Dark Tourism?" *The Observer*, October 23, 2005, http://tinyurl .com/24zsbk.

Lennon, J., and M. Foley, *Dark Tourism: The Attraction of Death and Disaster* (London: Continuum, 2000).

Pickover, C., *The Book of Black* (New York: Dover, 2013).

Rojek, C., *Ways of Seeing-Modern Transformations in Leisure and Travel* (London: Macmillan, 1993).

Seaton, A. V., "Thanatourism's Final Frontiers? Visits to Cemeteries, Churchyards and Funerary Sites as Sacred and Secular Pilgrimage," *Tourism Recreation Research* 27 (2002): 73–82.

"The Word: Dark Tourism," *New Scientist* 2597 (March 31, 2007): 50.

Yuill, S. M., *Dark Tourism: Understanding Visitor Motivation at Sites of Death and Disaster*, Master's Thesis, Texas A&M University, December 2003, http://tinyurl.com/9mzshah.

2002: Programmed Cell Death

Edmonds, M., "What Is Apoptosis?" HowStuffWorks.com, accessed April 20, 2015, tinyurl.com/phbzjo6.

Melino, G., and D. Vaux, eds., preface to *Cell Death* (Hoboken, NJ: Wiley, 2010).

Melino, G., D. Vaux, and J. Ameisen, "The Siren's Song: This Death that Makes Life Live," in *Cell Death* (Hoboken, NJ: Wiley, 2010).

>100 Trillion: Death of Universe

Adams, F., Laughlin, G., *The Five Ages of the Universe* (New York: Free Press, 2000).

Pickover, C., *The Physics Book* (New York: Sterling, 2011).

>100 Trillion: Quantum Resurrection

Cosmologists also refer to these brains as "freaky observers," in contrast to the traditional observers of the cosmos. Note that these brains need not require real biological bodies to support them. Debates continue as to what actually is a "typical" observer in an infinite universe. If some atoms in another universe briefly come together and look and think *exactly* like you, is it you? Random fluctuations could even lead to a new Big Bang.

Aczel, A, "The Higgs, Boltzmann Brains, and Monkeys Typing Hamlet," *Discover*, October 31, 2012, tinyurl.com/n82r9zt.

Banks, T., "Entropy and Initial Conditions in Cosmology," Cornell University Library, January 16, 2007, tinyurl.com/yjxapye.

Battersby, S. "Quantum Resurrection," sidebar in "The Final Unraveling of the Universe," *New Scientist*, 185(2005): 31-37.

Carroll, S., "The Higgs Boson vs. Boltzmann Brains," 2013, tinyurl.com/mnhkozc. "If the universe enters a de Sitter vacuum phase that is truly eternal, there will be a finite temperature in empty space and corresponding thermal fluctuations. Among these fluctuations will be intelligent observers. . . . "

Pickover, C., *The Physics Book* (New York: Sterling, 2011).

INDEX

IMAGE CREDITS

Because several of the old and rare illustrations shown in this book were difficult to acquire in a clean and legible form, I have sometimes taken the liberty to apply image-processing techniques to remove dirt and scratches, enhance faded portions, and occasionally add a slight coloration to a black-and-white figure in order to highlight details or to make an image more compelling. I hope that historical purists will forgive these slight artistic touches and understand that my goal was to create an attractive book that is aesthetically interesting for a wide audience. My fascination for the incredible depth and diversity of topics revolving around death and the afterlife should be evident through the photographs and drawings.